et pepper. When that was o
first tip,) we went out to t
at, papa?" said he, as we
I could record all his epo
worth writing down, till I
must be ... their
down ... say this
... a great picker!" He
him very ware; and this
you think I don't kn
"But I knew how to the
... did n't," rejoined he.
... of practical sagacity (h
... hit) to console him
... he has the stuff in him

*Twenty Days with
Julian & Little Bunny
By Papa*

The road to Lenox.

NATHANIEL HAWTHORNE

*Twenty Days with
Julian & Little Bunny
By Papa*

———

*Introduction by
Paul Auster*

NEW YORK REVIEW BOOKS, NEW YORK

This is a New York Review Book
Published by The New York Review of Books
1755 Broadway, New York, NY 10019

Library of Congress Cataloging-in-Publication Data
Hawthorne, Nathaniel, 1804–1864.
  Twenty days with Julian & Little Bunny by Papa / by Nathaniel Hawthorne ; introduction by Paul Auster.
    p. cm. — (New York Review Books classics)
  ISBN 1-59017-042-3 (alk. paper)
  1. Hawthorne, Nathaniel, 1804–1864—Diaries. 2. Hawthorne, Nathaniel, 1804–1864—Family. 3. Hawthorne, Julian, 1846–1934—Childhood and youth. 4. Fathers and sons—Massachusetts—History—19th century. 5. Authors, American—19th century—Diaries. I. Title: Twenty days with Julian and Little Bunny by Papa. II. Title. III. Series.
  PS1881.A3 2003
  813'.3—dc21   2003006574

Book design by Lizzie Scott
Printed in the United States of America on acid-free paper.
10 9 8 7 6 5 4 3 2 1

Endpapers: Manuscript page of "Twenty Days with Julian & Little Bunny by Papa." Collection of The Pierpont Morgan Library (MA 569)

June 2003
www.nyrb.com

INTRODUCTION

Twenty Days with Julian & Little Bunny by Papa is one of the least-known works by a well-known writer in all of literature. Buried in the seventh folio of Hawthorne's *American Notebooks*—that massive, little-read tome of treasures and revelations—the fifty pages that comprise this brief, self-contained narrative were written in Lenox, Massachusetts, between July 28 and August 16, 1851. In June of the previous year, Hawthorne and his wife had moved to a small red farmhouse in the Berkshires with their two children, Una (born in 1844) and Julian (born in 1846). A third child, Rose, was born in May 1851. A couple of months later, accompanied by her two daughters and her older sister, Elizabeth Peabody, Sophia Hawthorne left Lenox to visit her parents in West Newton, just outside Boston. Remaining in the house were Hawthorne, the five-year-old Julian, Mrs. Peters (the cook and housekeeper), and a pet rabbit who eventually came to be known as Hindlegs. That evening, after putting Julian to bed, Hawthorne sat down and wrote the first chapter of his little saga. With no intention other than to record the doings in the household during his wife's absence, he had inadvertently embarked on something that no writer had ever attempted before him: a meticulous, blow-by-blow account of a man taking care of a young child by himself.

In some ways, the situation is reminiscent of the old folk tale about the farmer and his wife who swap chores for a day. There are many versions of the story, but the outcome is always the same. The man, who has either belittled the woman for not working as hard as he does or scolded her for not doing her work well, makes a complete botch of it when he dons an apron and assumes the role of domestic manager. Depending on which variant you read, he either sets fire to the kitchen or winds up dangling from a rope attached to the family cow, who, after a long chain of misadventures, has managed to get herself onto the roof of the house. In all versions, it is the wife who comes to the rescue. Calmly planting crops in a nearby field, she hears her husband's screams and runs back home to extricate him from his predicament before he burns the place down or breaks his neck.

Hawthorne didn't break his neck, but he clearly felt that he was on rocky ground, and the tone of *Twenty*

Days is at once comic, self-deprecatory, and vaguely befuddled, shot through with what the grown-up Julian would later describe as his father's "humorous gravity." Readers familiar with the style of Hawthorne's stories and novels will be struck by the clarity and simplicity of expression in the *Notebooks*. The dark, brooding obsessions of his fiction produced a complex, often ornate density to his sentences, a refinement that sometimes bordered on the fussy or obscure, and some readers of his early tales (which were mostly published unsigned) mistakenly assumed that their author was a woman. Henry James, who wrote one of the first book-length studies of Hawthorne's work, learned much from this original and delicate prose, which was unique in its ability to join the intricacies of acute psychological observation with large moral and philosophical concerns. But James was not Hawthorne's only reader, and there are several other Hawthornes who have come down to us as well: Hawthorne the allegorist, Hawthorne the high Romantic fabulist, Hawthorne the chronicler of seventeenth-century colonial New England, and, most notably, Hawthorne as reimagined by Borges—the precursor of Kafka. Hawthorne's fiction can be read profitably from any one of these angles, but there is yet another Hawthorne who has been more or less forgotten, neglected because of the magnitude of his other achievements: the private Hawthorne, the scribbler of anecdotes and impulsive thoughts, the workman of ideas, the meteorologist and depictor of landscapes, the traveler, the letter-writer, the historian of everyday life. The pages of *The American Notebooks* are so fresh, so vivid in their articulations, that Hawthorne emerges from them not as some venerable figure from the literary past, but as a contemporary, a man whose time is still the present.

Twenty Days was not the only occasion on which he wrote about his children. Once Una and Julian were old enough to talk, he seemed to take immense pleasure in jotting down some of their zanier utterances, and the notebooks are studded with entries such as these:

> "I'm tired of all sings, and want to slip into God. I'm tired of little Una Hawsorne." "Are you tired of Mamma?" "No." "But you are tired of Papa?" "No." "I am tired of Dora, and tired of little Julian, and tired of little Una Hawsorne."

> Una—"You hurt me a little."
> Julian—"Well, I'll hurt you a big."

> Julian—"Mamma, why is not dinner supper?"— Mamma—"Why is not a chair a table?"—Julian— "Because it's a teapot."

I said to Julian, "Let me take off your bib"—and he taking no notice, I repeated it two or three times, each time louder than before. At last he bellowed—"Let me take off your Head!"

On Sunday, March 19, 1848, during the period when he was employed at the U.S. Custom House in Salem, Hawthorne spent the entire day recording the activities and antics of his two offspring—one just four and the other not quite two. It is a dizzying account of some nine pages that conscientiously takes note of every whim and twist of mood that occurred in the children over the course of eleven hours. Lacking the sentimental flourishes one might expect from a nineteenth-century parent, devoid of moralizing judgments or intrusive commentary, it stands as a remarkable portrait of the reality of childhood—which, on the strength of these passages, would seem to be eternal in its sameness:

Now Una offers her finger to Julian, and they march together, the little boy aping a manly measurement of stride. Now Una proposes to play Puss in the Corner; and there is a quick tatoo of little feet all over the floor. Julian utters a complaining cry about something or other—Una runs and kisses him. Una says, "Father—*this* morning, I am not going to be naughty at all." Now they are playing with India rubber balls. Julian tries to throw the ball into the air, but usually succeeds no farther than to drop it over his head. It rolls away—and he searches for it, inquiring—"where ball?" . . . Julian now falls into a reverie, for a little space—his mind seeming far away, lost in reminiscences;—but what can they be about? Recollections of a pre-existence. Now, he sits in his little chair, his chunky little figure looking like an alderman in miniature. . . . Mamma is dressing little Una in her purple pelisse, to go out with Dora. Una promises to be a very good little girl, and mind Dora—and not run away, nor step in the mud. The little boy trudges round, repeating "Go!—go!"—intimating his desire to be taken out likewise. He runs to-and-fro across the room, with a marvellous swagger—of the ludicrousness of which he seems perfectly conscious; and when I laugh, he comes to my elbow and looks up in my face, with a most humorous response. . . . He climbs into a chair at my knee, and peeps at himself in the glass—now he looks curiously on the page as I write—now, he nearly tumbles down, and is at first frightened—but, seeing that I was likewise startled, pretends to tumble again, and then laughs in my face. Enter mamma with the milk. His sits on his mother's knee, gulping the milk with grunts and sighs of satisfaction—nor ceases till the cup is exhausted, once, and again, and again—and even then asks for more. On being undressed, he is [taking an air-bath]— he enjoys the felicity of utter nakedness—running away from Mamma with cries of remonstrance, when she wishes to put on his night-gown. Now ensues a terrible catastrophe—not to be mentioned in our seemly history. . . . Enter Una—"Where is little Julian?" "He has gone out to walk." "No; but I mean where is the place of little Julian, that you've been writing about him." So I point to the page, at which she looks with all possible satisfaction; and stands watching the pen as it hurries forward. "I'll put the ink nearer to you," says she. "Father, are you going to write all this?" she adds, turning over the book. . . . I tell her that I am now writing about herself—"That's nice writing," says she. . . . Una now proposes to him to build a block house with her; so they set about it jointly; but it has scarcely risen above its founda- tion, before Julian tears it down. With unwearied patience, Una begins another. "Papa! 'Ouse!" cries Julian, pointing to two blocks which he has laid together. . . . They quit the blocks; and Julian again offers to climb the chair to the bookcase; and is again forbidden by me;—whereupon he cries—Una runs to kiss and comfort him—and then comes to me with a solemn remonstrance, of no small length; the burthen being, "Father, you should not speak so loudly to a little boy who is only half years old." . . . She comes and takes her place silently in my lap, resting her head on my shoulder. Julian has clambered into a chair at the window, and appears to observe and meditate; so that we have a very quiet interval, until he disturbs it by coming and pulling off her shoe. He seldom pretermits any mischief that his hand finds to do:—for instance, finding her bare knee, he has just taken occasion to pinch it with all his might. . . .

Hawthorne repeated the exercise four days later, on Thursday, March 23, and six times more in 1849, covering what would amount to another thirty pages in the Centenary Edition of the *Notebooks*. Adding to his descriptions of his children's games and squabbles and inner storms, he sometimes paused to make a number of more generalized remarks about their personalities. Two small passages about Una are of particular interest, since she is usually taken to be the model on which he based the character of Pearl in *The Scarlet Letter*. From January 28, 1849: "Her beauty is the most flitting, transitory, most uncertain and unaccountable affair, that ever had a real existence; it beams out when nobody expects it; it has mysteriously passed away, when you think yourself sure of it;—if you glance sideways at her, you perhaps think it is illuminating her face, but, turning full round to enjoy it, it is gone again. . . . When really visible, it is rare and precious as the vision of an angel; it is a transfiguration— a grace, delicacy, an ethereal fineness, which, at once, in my secret soul, makes me give up all severe opinions that I may have begun to form respecting her. It is but fair to conclude, that, on these occasions, we see her real soul; when she seems less lovely, we merely see something external. But, in truth, one manifestation belongs to her as much as another; for, before the establishment of principles, what is character but the series and succession of moods?" From July 30 of the same year: ". . . There is something that almost frightens me about the child—I know not whether elfish or angelic, but, at all events, supernatural. She steps so boldly into the midst of everything, shrinks from nothing, has such a comprehension of everything, seems at times to have but little delicacy, and anon shows that she possesses the finest essence of it; now so hard, now so tender; now so perfectly unreasonable, soon again so wise. In short, I now and then catch an aspect of her, in which I cannot believe her to be my own human child, but a spirit strangely mingled with good and evil, haunting the house where I dwell. The little boy is always the same child, and never varies in his relation to me."

By the summer of 1851, Hawthorne was a seasoned

observer of his own children, a veteran of family life. He was forty-seven years old and had been married for close to a decade. He couldn't have known it then, but nearly every important word of fiction he would ever publish had already been written. Behind him were the two editions of *Twice-Told Tales* (1837 and 1842), *Mosses from an Old Manse* (1846), and *The Snow-Image, and Other Twice-Told Tales* (already finished and planned for publication in late 1851)—his entire output as a writer of short stories. His first two novels had been published in 1850 and 1851. *The Scarlet Letter* had turned "the obscurest man of letters in America" into one of the most respected and celebrated writers of his time, and *The House of the Seven Gables* had only strengthened his reputation, prompting many critics to call him the finest writer the Republic had yet produced. Years of solitary labor had at last won him public reward, and after two decades of scrambling to make ends meet, 1851 marked the first year that Hawthorne earned enough from his writing to be able to support his family. Nor was there any reason to think that his success would not continue. Throughout the spring and early summer, he had written *A Wonder Book for Girls and Boys*, finishing the preface on July 15, just two weeks before Sophia's departure for West Newton, and he was already making plans for his next novel, *The Blithedale Romance*. Looking back on Hawthorne's career now, and knowing that he would be dead just thirteen years later (a few weeks short of his sixtieth birthday), that season in Lenox stands out as one of the happiest periods of his life, a moment of sublime equipoise and fulfillment. But it was nearly August now, and for many years Hawthorne had routinely suspended his literary work during the hot months. It was a time for loafing and reflection, in his opinion, a time for being outdoors, and he had always written as little as possible throughout the dog days of the New England summers. When he composed his little chronicle of the three weeks he spent with his son, he was not stealing time from other, more important projects. It was the only work he did, the only work he wanted to do.

The move to Lenox had been precipitated by Hawthorne's disastrous experiences in Salem in 1849. As he put it in a letter to his friend Horatio Bridge, he had come to dislike the town "so much that I hate to go into the streets, or to have the people see me. Anywhere else, I shall at once be entirely another man." Appointed to the post of surveyor in the Salem Custom House in 1846 during the Democratic administration of James Polk, Hawthorne accomplished almost nothing as a writer during the three years he held this job. With the election of Whig candidate Zachary Taylor in 1848, Hawthorne was sacked when the new administration took office in March 1849—but not without raising a great noise in his own defense, which led to a highly publicized controversy about the practice of political patronage in America. At the precise moment when this struggle was being waged, Hawthorne's mother died after a short illness. The notebook entries from those days in late July are among the most wrenching, emotionally charged paragraphs in all of Hawthorne. "Louisa pointed to a chair near the bed; but I was moved to kneel down close to my mother, and take her hand. She knew me, but could only murmur a few indistinct words—among which I understood an injunction to take care of my sisters. Mrs. Dike left the chamber, and then I found the tears slowly gathering in my eyes. I tried to keep them down; but it would not be—I kept filling up, till, for a few moments, I shook with sobs. For a long time, I knelt there, holding her hand; and surely it is the darkest hour I ever lived."

Ten days after his mother's death, Hawthorne lost his fight to save his job. Within days of his dismissal (perhaps even the same day, if family legend is to be believed), he began writing *The Scarlet Letter*, which was completed in six months. Under great financial strain during this period, his fortunes took a sudden, unexpected turn for the better just as plans were being made by the firm of Ticknor and Fields to publish the novel. By private, anonymous subscription, friends and supporters of Hawthorne (among them, most likely, Longfellow and Lowell) "who admire your genius and respect your character . . . [and to pay] the debt we owe you for what you have done for American literature" had raised the sum of five hundred dollars to help see Hawthorne through his difficulties. This windfall allowed Hawthorne to carry out his increasingly urgent desire to leave Salem, his hometown, and become "a citizen of somewhere else."

After a number of possibilities fell through (a farm in Manchester, New Hampshire, a house in Kittery, Maine), he and Sophia eventually settled on the red farmhouse in Lenox. It was, as Hawthorne put it to one of his former Custom House co-workers, "as red as the Scarlet Letter." Sophia was responsible for finding the place, which was situated on a larger property known as Highwood, currently being rented by the Tappan family. Mrs. Tappan, née Caroline Sturgis, was a friend of Sophia's, and it was she who offered the house to the Hawthornes—free of charge. Hawthorne, wary of the complications that might arise from living off the generosity of others, struck a bargain with Mr. Tappan to pay a nominal rent of seventy-five dollars for four years.

One would assume that he was satisfied with the arrangement, but that didn't stop him from grumbling about any number of petty annoyances. No sooner did the family settle into the house than Hawthorne came down with a bad cold, which confined him to bed for several days, and before long he was complaining in a letter to his sister Louisa that the farmhouse was "the most inconvenient and wretched little hovel that I ever put my head in." (Even the optimistic Sophia, who tended to see every adversity in the best possible light, admitted in a letter to her mother that is was "the smallest of ten-foot houses"— barely adequate for a family of four, let alone five.) If the house displeased Hawthorne, he had even harsher things to say about the landscape that surrounded it. Sixteen months after moving in, he wrote to his publisher, James T. Fields, that "I have staid here too long and too constantly. To tell you a secret, I am sick to death of Berkshire, and hate to think of spending another winter here. . . . The air and climate do not agree with my health at all; and, for the first time since I was a boy, I have felt languid and dispirited, during almost my whole residence here. Oh that Providence would build me the merest little shanty, and mark me out a rood or two of garden-ground, near the sea-coast." Two years later, long after he had moved away and resettled in Concord, he was still grinding the same axe, as shown in this passage from the introduction to *Tanglewood Tales* (a second volume of Greek myths for children): "But, to me, there is a peculiar, quiet charm in these broad meadows and gentle eminences. They are better than mountains, because they do not stamp and stereotype themselves into the brain, and thus grow wearisome with the same strong impression, repeated day after day. A few summer weeks among mountains; a lifetime among green meadows and placid slopes, with outlines forever new, because continually fading out of the memory. Such would be my sober choice." It is ironic that the area around Lenox should still be referred to as "Tanglewood." The word was Hawthorne's invention and is now indelibly associated with the music festival that takes place there every year. For a man who hated the area and ran away from it after just eighteen months, he left his mark on it forever.

Still, it was the best moment of his life, whether he knew it or not. Solvent, successfully married to an intelligent and famously devoted woman, in the middle of the most prolific writing burst of his career, Hawthorne planted his vegetable garden, fed his chickens, and played with his children in the afternoon. The shyest and most reclusive of men, known for his habit of hiding behind rocks and trees to avoid talking to people he knew, Hawthorne largely kept to himself during his stint in the Berkshires, avoiding the social activities of the local gentry and appearing in town only to collect his mail at the post office and return home. Solitude was his natural element, and considering the circumstances of his life until his early thirties, it was remarkable that he had married at all. When you were a person whose ship-captain father had died in Surinam when you were four, when you had grown up with a remote and elusive mother who had lived in a state of permanent, isolated widowhood, when you had served what is probably the most stringent literary apprenticeship on record—locking yourself up in your room for twelve years in a house you had dubbed "Castle Dismal" and leaving Salem only in the summer to go on solitary rambles through the New England countryside—then perhaps the society of your immediate family was sufficient. Hawthorne had married late to a woman who had likewise married late, and in the twenty-two years they lived together, they were rarely apart. He called her Phoebe, Dove, Beloved, Dearissima, Ownest One. "Sometimes (for I had no wife then to keep my heart warm)," he had written to her during their courtship in 1840, "it seemed as if I were already in the grave, with only life enough to be chilled and benumbed . . . till at length a certain Dove was revealed to me, in the shadow of a seclusion as deep as my own had been. And I drew nearer and nearer to the Dove, and opened my bosom to her . . . keeping my heart warm, and renewing my life with her own. . . . Thou only hast taught me that I have a heart—thou only hast thrown a light deep downward, and upward, into my soul. Thou only hast revealed me to myself; for without thy aid, my best knowledge of myself would have been merely to know my own shadow—to watch it flickering on the wall, and mistake its fantasies for my own real actions. . . . Now, dearest, dost thou comprehend what thou hast done for me?"

They lived in isolation, but visitors nevertheless came (relatives, old friends), and they were in contact with several of their neighbors. One of them, who lived six miles down the road in Pittsfield, was Herman Melville, then thirty-two years old. Much has been written about the relationship between the two writers (some of it pertinent, some of it nonsense), but it is clear that Hawthorne opened up to the younger Melville with unaccustomed enthusiasm and took great pleasure in his company. As he wrote to his friend Bridge on August 7, 1850: "I met Melville, the other day, and liked him so much that I have asked him to spend a few days with me before leaving these parts." Melville had only been visiting the area at the time, but by October he was back, acquiring the property in Pittsfield he renamed Arrowhead and installing himself in the Berkshires as a full-time resident. Over the next thirteen months, the two men talked, corresponded, and read each other's work, occasionally traveling the six miles between them to stay as a guest at the other's house. "Nothing pleases me more," Sophia wrote to her sister Elizabeth about the friendship between her husband and Melville (whom she playfully referred to as Mr. Omoo), "than to sit & hear this growing man dash his tumultuous waves of thought against Mr. Hawthorne's great, genial, comprehending silences. . . . Without doing anything on his own, except merely *being*, it is astonishing how people make him their innermost Father Confessor." For Melville, the encounter with Hawthorne and his writings marked a fundamental turn in his life. He had already begun his story about the white whale at the time of their first meeting (projected as a conventional high-seas adventure novel), but under Hawthorne's influence the book began to change and deepen and expand, transforming itself in an unabated frenzy of inspiration into the richest of all American novels, *Moby-Dick*. As everyone who has read the book knows, the first page reads: "In token of my admiration for his genius this book is inscribed to Nathaniel Hawthorne." Even if Hawthorne had accomplished nothing else during his stay in Lenox, he unwittingly served as Melville's muse.

The lease was good for four years, but shortly after the completion of *Twenty Days* and Sophia's return from West Newton with Una and baby Rose, Hawthorne contrived to get himself into a dispute with his landlords over a trivial matter of boundaries. The issue revolved around the question of whether he and his family had the right to pick the fruits and berries from the trees and bushes on the property. In a long, hilariously acidic letter to Mrs. Tappan dated September 5, 1851, Hawthorne set forth his case, concluding with a rather nasty challenge: "At any rate, take what you want, and that speedily, or there will be little else than a parcel of rotten plums to dispute about." A gracious, conciliatory letter from Mr. Tappan the following day—which Sophia characterized to her sister as "noble and beautiful" —seemed to settle the matter once and for all, but by then Hawthorne had already made up his mind to move, and the family soon packed up their belongings and were gone from the house on November 21.

Just one week earlier, on November 14, Melville had received his first copies of *Moby-Dick*. That same day, he drove his wagon over to the red farmhouse and invited Hawthorne to a farewell dinner at Curtis's Hotel in Lenox, where he presented his friend with a copy of the book. Until then, Hawthorne had known nothing about the effusive dedication to him, and while there is no record of his reaction to this unexpected tribute to "his genius," one can only surmise that he was deeply moved. Moved enough, in any case, to begin reading the book immediately upon returning home, surrounded by the chaos of boxes and packing crates as his family prepared for their departure. He must have read the book quickly and intensely, for his letter of response reached Melville on the sixteenth. All but one of Hawthorne's letters to Melville have been lost, but numerous letters from Melville to Hawthorne have survived, and his answer to this one is among the most memorable and frequently quoted letters in all of American literature: ". . . A sense of unspeakable security is in me this moment, on account of your having understood the book. I have written a wicked book, and feel spotless as the lamb. Ineffable socialities are in me. I would sit down and dine with you and all the gods in old Rome's Pantheon.... Whence come you, Hawthorne? By what right do you drink from the flagon of my life? And when I put it to my lips— lo, they are yours and not mine. I feel that the Godhead is broken up like the bread at the Supper, and that we are the pieces. Hence this infinite fraternity of feeling.... I shall leave the world, I feel, with more satisfaction for having come to know you. Knowing you persuades me more than the Bible of our immortality."

Melville makes a couple of appearances in *Twenty Days with Julian & Little Bunny*, but the gist of the piece is the little boy himself, the daily activities of father and son, the ephemeral nothings of domestic life. No dramas are reported, the routine is fairly monotonous, and in terms of content, one can hardly imagine a duller or more pedestrian undertaking. Hawthorne kept the diary for Sophia. It was written in a separate family notebook which they both used to record material about the children (and which the children had access to as well, sometimes adding drawings and infant scribbles of their own—and, in a few instances, even tracing their pencils directly over texts written by their parents). Hawthorne intended his wife to read the little work after her return from West Newton, and it appears that she did so at the earliest opportunity. Describing the trip home to Lenox in a letter to her mother three days later (August 19, 1851), Sophia wrote, "... Una was very tired, and her eyes looked as cavernous as Daniel Webster's till she saw the red house; and then she began to shout, and clap her hands for joy. Mr. Hawthorne came forth with a thousand welcomes in his eyes, and Julian leaped like a fountain, and was as impossible to hold fast.... I found that Mr. Hawthorne had written a minute account of his and Julian's life from the hour of our departure. He had a tea-party of New York gentlemen one day, and they took him and Julian on a long drive; and they all had a picnic together, and did not get home till eight o'clock. Mr. Melville came with these gentlemen, and once before in my absence. Mr. Hawthorne also had a visit from a Quaker lady of Philadelphia, Elizabeth Lloyd, who came to see the author of 'The Scarlet Letter.' He said that it was a very pleasant call. Mr. [G. P. R.] James also came twice, once with a great part of his family, once in a storm. Julian's talk flowed like a babbling brook, he writes, the whole three weeks, through all his meditations and reading. They spent a great deal of time at the lakes, and put Nat's ship out to sea.... Sometimes Julian pensively yearned for mama, but was not once out of temper or unhappy. There is a charming history of poor little Bunny, who died the morning of the day we returned. It did not appear why he should die, unless he lapped water off the bathing-room floor. But he was found stark and stiff. Mrs. Peters was very smiling, and grimly glad to see me...."

After Hawthorne's death in 1864, Sophia was prevailed upon by James T. Fields, Hawthorne's publisher and also the editor of the *Atlantic Monthly*, to choose excerpts from her husband's notebooks for publication in the magazine. Passages appeared in twelve successive issues in 1866, but when it came to *Twenty Days with Julian & Little Bunny*, which Fields was hoping to include, she hesitated, claiming that Julian would have to be consulted first. Her son apparently had no objections, but still Sophia was reluctant to give her consent, and after some further reflection she decided against printing the material, explaining to Fields that Hawthorne "would never have wished such an intimate domestic history to be made public, and I am astonished at myself that I ever thought of it." In 1884, when Julian published his own book, *Nathaniel Hawthorne and His Wife*, he included a number of extracts from *Twenty Days*, commenting that the three weeks he spent alone with his father "must have been weary work, sometimes, for Hawthorne, though for the little boy it was one uninterrupted succession of halcyon days." He mentions that a full version of the diary would make "as unique and quaint a little history as was ever seen," but it wasn't until 1932, when Randall Stewart put together the first scholarly edition of *The American Notebooks*, that *Twenty Days with Julian & Little Bunny* was finally made available to the public. Not as a separate book (as Julian had suggested) but as one section in a lengthy volume of eight hundred pages that spans the years 1835 to 1853.

Why publish it now as an independent work? Why should this small, uneventful piece of prose command our interest more than 150 years after it was written? I wish I could mount a cogent defense on its behalf, make some dazzling, sophisticated argument that would prove its greatness, but if the piece is great, it is great only in miniature, great only because the writing, in and of itself, gives pleasure. *Twenty Days* is a humorous work by a notoriously melancholic man, and anyone who has ever spent an extended length of time in the company of a small child will surely respond to the accuracy and honesty of Hawthorne's account.

Una and Julian were raised in an unorthodox manner, even by the standards of mid-nineteenth-century Transcendentalist New England. Although they reached school age during their time in Lenox, neither one was sent to school, and they spent their days at home with their mother, who took charge of their education and rarely allowed them to mingle with other children. The hermetic, Eden-like atmosphere that Hawthorne and Sophia tried to establish in Concord after their marriage apparently continued after they became parents. Writing to her mother from Lenox, Sophia eloquently delineated her philosophy of child-rearing: "... Alas for those who counsel sternness and severity instead of love towards their young children! How little they are like God, how much they are like Solomon, whom I really believe many persons prefer to imitate, and think they do well. Infinite patience, infinite tenderness, infinite magnanimity,—no less will do, and we must prac- tise them as far as finite power will allow. Above all, no parent should feel a *pride of power*. This, I doubt not, is the great stumbling-block, and it should never be indulged. From this comes the sharp rebuke, the cruel blow, the anger. A tender sorrow, a most sympathizing regret, alone should appear at the transgression of a child. ... Yet how immitigable is the judgment and treatment of these little misdemeanors often! When my children disobey, I am not personally aggrieved, and they see it, and find therefore that it is a disinterested desire that they should do right that induces me to insist. There is all the difference in the world between indulgence and tenderness."

Hawthorne, who acceded to his wife in all family and household matters, took a far less active role in raising the children. "If only papa wouldn't write, how nice it would be," Julian quoted Una as having declared one day, and according to him, "their feeling about all their father's writings was, that he was being wasted in his study, when

he might be with them, and there could be nothing in any books, whether his own or other authors', that could for a moment bear comparison with his actual companionship." When he finished working for the day, it seems that Hawthorne preferred acting as playmate with his children than as classic paternal figure. "Our father was a great tree-climber," Julian recalled, "and he was also fond of playing the magician. 'Hide your eyes!' he would say, and the next moment, from being there beside us on the moss, we would hear his voice descending from the sky, and behold! he swung among the topmost branches, showering down upon us a hail-storm of nuts." In her numerous letters and journal entries from that period, Sophia frequently noted glimpses of Hawthorne alone with the two children. "Mr. Hawthorne," she informed her mother, "has been lying down in the sunshine, slightly fleckered with the shadows of a tree, and Una and Julian have been making him look like the mighty Pan by covering his chin and breast with long grass-blades, that looked like a verdant, venerable beard." And again to her mother several days later: "Dear little harp-souled Una—whose love for her father grows more profound every day . . . was made quite unhappy because he did not go at the same time with her to the lake. His absence darkened all the sunshine to her; and when I asked her why she could not enjoy the walk as Julian did, she replied, 'Ah, *he* does not love papa as *I* do!' . . . After I put Julian to bed, I went out to the barn to see about the chickens, and she wished to go. There sat papa on the hay, and like a needle to a magnet she was drawn, and begged to see papa a little longer, and stay with him. Now she has come, weary enough; and after steeping her spirit in this rose and gold of twilight, she has gone to bed. With such a father, and such a scene before her eyes, and *with eyes to see*, what may we not hope of her? I heard her and Julian talking together about their father's smile, the other day—They had been speaking of some other person's smile—Mr. Tappan's, I believe; and presently Una said, 'But you know, Julian, that there is no smile like papa's!' 'Oh no,' replied Julian. 'Not like *papa's!*' " In 1904, many years after Una's early death at the age of thirty-three, Thomas Wentworth Higginson published a memorial piece about her in *The Outlook*, a popular magazine of the period. In it, he quoted her as once having said to him about her father: "He was capable of being the gayest person I ever saw. He was like a boy. Never was such a playmate as he in all the world."

All this lies behind the spirit of *Twenty Days with Julian & Little Bunny*. The Hawthornes were a consciously progressive family, and for the most part their treatment of their children corresponds to attitudes prevalent among the secular middle-class in America today. No harsh discipline, no physical punishment, no strident reprimands.

Some people found the Hawthorne children obstreperous and unruly, but Sophia, ever inclined to see them as model creatures, happily reported in a letter to her mother that at a local torchlight festival "the children enjoyed themselves extremely, and behaved so beautifully that they won all hearts. They thought that there never was such a superb child as Julian, nor such a grace as Una. 'They are neither too shy, nor bold,' said Mrs. Field, 'but just right.' " What constitutes "just right," of course, is a matter of opinion. Hawthorne, who was always more rigorous in his observations than his wife—unable, by force of instinct and habit, to allow love to color his judgments—makes no bones about how annoying Julian's presence sometimes was to him. That theme is sounded on the first page of the diary, and it recurs repeatedly throughout the twenty days they spent together. The boy was a champion chatterbox, a pint-sized engine of logorrhea, and within hours of Sophia's departure, Hawthorne was already complaining that "it is impossible to write, read, think, or even to sleep (in the daytime) so constant are his appeals to me in one way or another." By the second evening, after remarking once again on the endless stream of babble that issued from Julian's lips, Hawthorne put him to bed and added: "Nor need I hesitate to say that I was glad to get rid of him— it being my first relief from his society during the whole day. This may be too much of a good thing." Five days later,

on August 3, he was again harping on the same subject: "Either I have less patience to-day than ordinary, or the little man makes larger demands upon it; but it really does seem as if he had baited me with more questions, references, and observations, than mortal father ought to be expected to endure." And again on August 5: "He continues to pester me with his inquisitions. For instance, just now, while he is whittling with my jack-knife. 'Father, if you had bought all the jack-knives at the shop, what would you do for another, when you broke them all?' 'I would go somewhere else,' say I. But there is no stumping him so. 'If you had bought all the jack-knives in the world, what would you do?' And here my patience gives way, and I entreat him not to trouble me with any more foolish questions. I really think it would do him good to spank him, apropos to this habit." And once again on August 10: "Mercy on me, was ever man before so be-pelted with a child's talk as I am!"

These little bursts of irritation are precisely what give the text its charm—and its truth. No sane person can endure the company of a high-voltage child without an occasional meltdown, and Hawthorne's admissions of less-than-perfect calm turn the diary into something more than just a personal album of summer memories. There is sweetness in the text, to be sure, but it is never cloying (too much wit, too much bite), and because Hawthorne

refrains from glossing over his own faults and downcast moments, he takes us beyond a strictly private space into something more universal, more human. Again and again, he curbs his temper whenever he is on the verge of losing it, and the talk of spanking the boy is no more than a passing impulse, a way of letting off steam with his pen instead of his hand. By and large, he shows remarkable forbearance in dealing with Julian, indulging the five-year-old in his whims and escapades and cockeyed discourses with steadfast equanimity, readily allowing that "he is such a genial and good-humored little man that there is certainly an enjoyment intermixed with all the annoyance." In spite of the difficulties and possible frustrations, Hawthorne was determined not to rein in his son too tightly. After the birth of Rose in May, Julian had been forced to tiptoe around the house and speak in whispers. Now, suddenly, he is permitted to "shout and squeal just as loud as I please," and the father sympathizes with the boy's craving for commotion. "He enjoys this freedom so greatly," Hawthorne writes on the second day, "that I do not mean to restrain him, whatever noise he makes."

Julian was not the only source of irritation, however. On July 29, the wifeless husband unexpectedly exploded, blasting forth with a splenetic tirade on one of his constant obsessions: "This is a horrible, most hor-ri-ble climate; one knows not, for ten minutes together, whether he is too cool

or too warm; but he is always one or the other; and the constant result is a miserable disturbance of the system. I detest it! I detest it!! I de-test it!!! I hate Berkshire with my whole soul, and would joyfully see its mountains laid flat." On August 8, after an excursion with Melville and others to the Shaker community in nearby Hancock, he had nothing but the most vicious and cutting remarks to offer about the sect: "... All their miserable pretence of cleanliness and neatness is the thinnest superficiality... the Shakers are and must needs be a filthy set. And then their utter and systematic lack of privacy; their close junction of man with man [two men routinely slept in one small bed], and supervision of one man over another—it is hateful and disgusting to think of; and the sooner the sect is extinct the better. ..." Then, with a kind of gloating sarcasm, he applauds Julian for answering a call of nature during their visit and defecating on the property. "All through this outlandish village went our little man hopping and dancing, in excellent spirits; nor had he been long there before he desired to confer with himself—neither was I unwilling that he should bestow such a mark of his consideration (being the one of which they were most worthy) on the system and establishment of these foolish Shakers." Less severely, perhaps, but with a noticeable touch of disdain, he also had some unkind things to say about his neighbor and landlady, Caroline Tappan—a good month before the infamous fruit-

tree controversy, which would suggest a prior antipathy, perhaps one of long standing. (Some biographers have speculated that she made a pass at Hawthorne during Sophia's absence—or at least would have been willing to do so if he had given her any encouragement.) Hawthorne and Julian had given the pet rabbit to the Tappans, thinking the animal might be happier in the larger house, but for various reasons (a threatening dog, mistreatment by the Tappans' young daughter) the new arrangement had not worked out. Mrs. Tappan came to Hawthorne and "spoke of giving him to little Marshall Butler, and suggested, moreover (in reply to something that I said about putting him out of existence) that he might be turned out into the woods, to shift for himself. There is something characteristic in this idea; it shows the sort of sensitiveness, that finds the pain and misery of other people disagreeable, just as it would a bad scent, but is perfectly at ease when once they are removed from her sphere. I suppose she would not for the world have killed Bunny, although she would have exposed him to the certainty of lingering starvation, without scruple or remorse."

Apart from these rare instances of pique and outrage, the atmosphere of *Twenty Days* is serene, measured, bucolic. Every morning, Hawthorne and Julian went to fetch milk at a neighboring farm; they engaged in "sham-battles," collected the mail at the Lenox post office in the afternoon, and made frequent trips to the lake. On the way, they "waged war with the thistles," which was Julian's favorite sport—pretending that the thistles were dragons and beating them heartily with sticks. They collected flowers, gathered currants, and picked green beans and summer squashes from the garden. Hawthorne built a makeshift boat for Julian, using a newspaper as a sail; a drowning cat was saved from a cistern; and during their visits to the lake, they variously fished, flung stones into the water, and dug in the sand. Hawthorne gave Julian a bath every morning and then wrestled with the task of trying to curl his hair, seldom with satisfactory results. There was a bed-wetting accident on August 3, a painful wasp sting on the 5th, a stomachache and a headache to be attended to on the 13th and 14th, and an untimely loss of bladder control during a walk home on the 6th, which prompted Hawthorne to remark, "I heard him squealing, while I was some distance behind; and approaching nearer, I saw that he walked wide between the legs. Poor little man! His drawers were all a-sop." Even if he wasn't completely at home with the job, the father had little by little become the mother, and by August 12 we understand how thoroughly Hawthorne had assumed this role when, for the first time in more than two weeks, he suddenly lost track of where Julian was. "After dinner, I sat down with a book . . . and . . . he was absent in parts unknown, for the

space of an hour. At last I began to think it time to look him up; for, now that I am alone with him, I have all his mother's anxieties, added to my own. So I went to the barn, and to the currant-bushes, and shouted around the house, without response, and finally sat down on the hay, not knowing which way to seek him. But by and by, he ran round the house, holding up his little fist, with a smiling phiz, and crying out that he had something very good for me."

Barring the excursion to the Shaker Village with Melville on August 8, the pair stayed close to home, but that outing proved to be an exhilarating experience for the little boy, and Hawthorne is at his best in capturing his enthusiasm, in being able to see the event through his son's eyes. The group lost its way on the carriage ride home, and by the time they passed through Lenox, "it was beyond twilight; indeed, but for the full moon, it would have been quite dark. The little man behaved himself still like an old traveller; but sometimes he looked round at me from the front seat (where he sat between Herman Melville and Evert Duyckinck) and smiled at me with a peculiar expression, and put back his hand to touch me. It was a method of establishing a sympathy in what doubtless appeared to him the wildest and unprecedentedest series of adventures that had ever befallen mortal travellers."

The next morning, Julian announced to Hawthorne that

he loved Mr. Melville as much as his father, his mother, and Una, and based on the evidence of a short letter that Melville sent to Julian six months later (long after the Hawthornes had left the Berkshires), it would appear that this fondness was reciprocated. "I am very happy that I have a place in the heart of so fine a little fellow as you," he wrote, and then, after commenting on the heavy snow-drifts in the woods around Pittsfield, concluded with a warm valediction: "Remember me kindly to your good father, Master Julian, and Good Bye, and may Heaven always bless you, & may you be a good boy and become a great good man."

An earlier visit from Melville to Lenox on August 1 (his thirty-second birthday) provided Hawthorne with what were probably his most pleasurable hours during those three weeks of bachelor life. After stopping in at the post office with Julian that afternoon, he paused on the way home in a secluded spot to read his newspapers when "a cavalier on horseback came along the road, and saluted me in Spanish; to which I replied by touching my hat, and went on with the newspaper. But the cavalier renewing his salutation, I regarded him more attentively, and saw that it was Herman Melville!" The two men walked the mile to the red house together (with Julian, "highly pleased," sitting atop Melville's horse), and then, in what are probably the most frequently quoted sentences from *The American*

Notebooks, Hawthorne continues: "After supper, I put Julian to bed; and Melville and I had a talk about time and eternity, things of this world and of the next, and books, and publishers, and all possible and impossible matters, that lasted pretty deep into the night; and if truth must be told, we smoked cigars even within the sacred precincts of the sitting-room. At last, he arose, and saddled his horse (whom we had put into the barn) and rode off for his own domicile; and I hastened to make the most of what little sleeping-time remained for me."

That was the one galvanizing moment in an otherwise torpid stretch of days. When he wasn't taking care of Julian, Hawthorne wrote letters, read Fourier as he prepared to begin *The Blithedale Romance*, and took a halfhearted stab at Thackeray's *Pendennis*. The diary includes many keenly written passages about the shifting light of the landscape (few novelists looked at nature as attentively as Hawthorne did) and a handful of droll and increasingly sympathetic descriptions of Hindlegs, the pet rabbit, who unfortunately expired as the chronicle was coming to an end. More and more, however, as his solitude dragged on, Hawthorne yearned for his wife to come home. By the beginning of the final week, that feeling had been turned into a constant ache. After putting Julian to bed on the evening of August 10, he suddenly let himself go, breaking down in a rhapsodic gush of longing and allegiance. "Let me say outright, for once, that he is a sweet and lovely little boy, and worthy of all the love that I am capable of giving him. Thank God! God bless him! God bless Phoebe for giving him to me! God bless her as the best wife and mother in the world! God bless Una, whom I long to see again! God bless Little Rosebud! God bless me, for Phoebe's and all their sakes! No other man has so good a wife; nobody has better children. Would I were worthier of her and them!" The entry then concludes: "My evenings are all dreary, alone, and without books that I am in the mood to read; and this evening was like the rest. So I went to bed at about nine, and longed for Phoebe."

He was expecting her to return on the 13th, then on the 14th, then on the 15th, but various delays and missed communications put off Sophia's departure from West Newton until the 16th. Increasingly anxious and frustrated, Hawthorne nevertheless pushed on dutifully with the diary. On the very last day, during yet another visit to the lake with Julian, he sat down at the edge of the water with a magazine, and as he read, he was moved to make the following observation, which in some sense stands as a brief and inadvertent *ars poetica*, a precise description of the spirit and methodology of all his writing: ". . . The best way to get a vivid impression and feeling of a landscape, is to sit down before it and read, or become otherwise absorbed in thought; for then, when your eyes happen to be attracted to the landscape, you seem to catch Nature at unawares, and see her before she has time to change her aspect. The effect lasts but for a single instant, and passes away almost as soon as you are conscious of it; but it is real, for that moment. It is as if you could overhear and understand what the trees are whispering to one another; as if you caught a glimpse of a face unveiled, which veils itself from every wilful glance. The mystery is revealed, and after a breath or two, becomes just as much a mystery as before."

As with landscapes, so with people, especially little people in the flush of childhood. All is change with them, all is movement, and you can grasp their essence only "at unawares," at moments when you are not consciously looking for it. That is the beauty of Hawthorne's little piece of notebook-writing. Throughout all the drudgery and tedium of his constant companionship with the five-year-old boy, Hawthorne was able to glance at him often enough to capture something of his essence, to bring him to life in words. A century and a half later, we are still trying to discover our children, but these days we do it by taking snapshots and following them around with video cameras. But words are better, I think, if only because they don't fade with time. It takes more effort to write a truthful sentence than to focus a lens and push a button, of course, but words go deeper than pictures do—which can rarely record anything more than the surfaces of things, whether landscapes or the faces of children. In all but the best or luckiest photographs, the soul is missing. That is why *Twenty Days with Julian & Little Bunny* merits our attention. In his modest, deadpan way, Hawthorne managed to accomplish what every parent dreams of doing: to keep his child alive forever.

—PAUL AUSTER
July 2002

At seven o'clock A. M. wife, E.P.P., Una, and Rosebud, took their departure, leaving Julian and me in possession of the Red Shanty. (The first observation which the old gentleman made thereupon was — "Papa, is it not nice to have her by gone?" This perfect confidence of my sympathy in this feeling was very queer." "Why is it nice?" I enquired. "Because now I can howl and squeal just as bad as I please!" answered he. And for the next half hour he exercised his lungs to his heart's content, and almost split the welkin thereby. Then he hammered on an empty box, and appeared to have high enjoyment of the racket which he created. In the course of the afternoon, however, he fell into a deep reverie, and looked very pensive. I asked what he was thinking of, and he said "Oh, about mamma's going away. I do not like to be away from her," and then he communicated about getting horses and following after her. He declared, likewise, that he likes Lenox, and that he never travelled.

I hardly know how we got through the fore-noon ~~———————————————————— ————————————————————~~. It is impossible to write, read, think, or even to sleep (in the daytime) so constant are his appeals to me in one way or another; till he is in such a pitiful need I find him such little use that there is certainly a sunniness intermixed with all the annoyance.

In the afternoon we walked down to the lake, and amused ourself with flinging in stones, until the gathering clouds warned us homeward. On the wood-ward, mid-way home, a shower overtook us; and we sat on an old decayed log, while the drops pattered plentifully on the trees overhead. He enjoyed the shower, and favored me with a great many wise other-wise remarks.) ~~———————————————— ———————————————————————~~

First page of the manuscript of "Twenty Days with Julian & Little Bunny by Papa" in the Hawthorne family album.

to send one of the copies of the biography to
Nathaniel in my bundle this afternoon.
Little Rose fell down & bumped her angel
head very hard so that there was a great
swell. It frightened Fullen so much as to
make her headache very badly so I had to
give her opium. Arnica soon relieved the
blue bruise, but she cried piteously. Baby
has made great progress in words. She says
a great many very well. Ellen has talked
to me all the evening & it is very late. I must
go to bed — my eyes are shut. It is not of
much use to write such skeletons.

Sept. 15. Wednesday. No dear husband to day. The
children are getting very impatient, & Julian
jumps to the ceiling at every car whistle,
so sure it brings Papa. Una this afternoon cleared
up the dining room for Mamma, & went into the
study & raised the curtains, & the tea roses
there were perfuming the room. She thought
Papa might come at five o'clock. But the rain
cleared & the golden sunset came, but our
sun did not come. Never was father never
was husband so loved & longed for. We have not
been able to get the mail to-day, on account of
the rain. Perhaps there is a letter from him.
It is starlight now & we can send tomorrow.
Julian has spelled words on the black board to
day & drawn astonishing vases. Una drew
a beautiful vase & tried to draw the lamp too
for her lesson. Then she learned a Botany
lesson & spelled & learned a Poem —
I was very much struck with Julian's conscience
to-day. He came up stairs when I was dressing
my hair, & said Una was very wrong, for she
had been telling baby that if she would hug
her round the neck, she would put her on the
couch. He thought it was bribery, & knowing it
was not my practice, he thought there was a
transgression. I was very much impressed with the
nicety of his fidelity — It is so with Julian. He gets an
idea of a matter & it is very clearly comprehended,
though he does make funny blunders about material

We went to the lake, in accordance with the old boy's wish. He had taken with him the little vessel that his uncle Pat made for him, long ago, and which, since yesterday, has been his favorite plaything. He launched it upon the lake, and it looked very like a real sloop, tossing up and down on the swelling waves. I believe he would very contentedly have spent a hundred years, or so, with no other amusement than this. Meanwhile, took the Montreal tea from my pocket and penciled a pretty attentive perusal. I have before now experienced, that the best way to get a vivid impression and feeling of a landscape, is to sit down before it and read, or become otherwise absorbed in thought; for then, when your eyes happen to be attracted to the landscape, you seem to catch Nature at unawares, and see her before she has time to change her aspect. The effect lasts but for a single instant, and passes away almost as soon as you are conscious of it; but it is real, for that moment. It is as if you could overhear and understand what the trees are whispering to one another; as if you caught a glimpse of a face unveiled, which hides itself from every wilful glance. The mystery is revealed, and, after a breath or two, becomes just as much a mystery as before. I caught one such glimpse, this afternoon, though not so perfectly as sometimes. It was half past twelve when we got back.

(I forgot to say that I left a note for Mr. Keeler, at the Post office, requesting him to wait in Pittsfield for O'Toole.) If they do not come to-day, — well, I don't know what I shall do.

It is nearly six by the clock, and they do not come! Surely they must, must, must be here to-night!

Within a quarter of an hour after writing the above, they here came — all well! Thank God.

Last page of the manuscript.

Julian and Una.
Daguerrotype, c. 1848–49.

Sophia Peabody.
Engraving by Schoff
from a portrait
presumably painted
by Chester Harding.

Hawthorne at 36.
Portrait by Charles
Osgood, 1840.

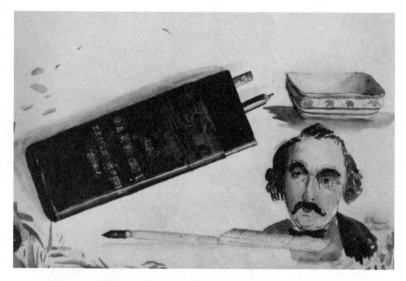

Sketch of Nathaniel Hawthorne by Julian, 1859.

*Twenty Days with
Julian & Little Bunny
By Papa*

LENOX, MONDAY, JULY 28TH, 1851.

———

At seven o'clock, A.M. Wife, E. P. P., Una, and Rosebud, took their departure, leaving Julian and me in possession of the Red Shanty. The first observation which the old gentleman made thereupon, was—"Father, isn't it nice to have baby gone?" His perfect confidence of my sympathy in this feeling was very queer. "Why is it nice?" I inquired. "Because now I can shout and squeal just as loud as I please!" answered he. And for the next half hour he exercised his lungs to his heart's content, and almost split the welkin thereby. Then he hammered on an empty box, and appeared to have high enjoyment of the racket which he created. In the course of the forenoon, however, he fell into a deep reverie, and looked very pensive. I asked what he was thinking of, and he said, "Oh, about Mama's going away. I do not like to be away from her;"—and then he romanticized about getting horses and galloping after her. He declared, likewise, that he likes Una, and that she never troubled him. [. . .]

I hardly know how we got through the forenoon-bath; [. . .], and [. . .] [such] kinds of rational employment. It is impossible to write, read, think, or even to sleep (in the daytime) so constant are his appeals to me in one way or another; still he is such a genial and good-humored little man that there is certainly an enjoyment intermixed with all the annoyance.

In the afternoon we walked down to the lake, and amused ourself with flinging in stones, until the gathering clouds warned us homeward. In the wood, mid-way home, a shower overtook us; and we sat on an old decayed log, while the drops pattered plentifully on the trees overhead. He enjoyed the shower, and favored me with a great many weatherwise remarks, for it is to be observed, that he has a marvellous opinion of his own wisdom, and thinks himself beyond a comparison sager and more experienced than his father. It continued showery all the rest of the day; so that I do not recollect of his going out afterwards.

For an in-door playmate, there was Bunny, who does not turn out to be a very interesting companion, and makes me more trouble than he is worth. There ought to be two rabbits, in order to bring out each other's remarkable qualities—if any there be. Undoubtedly, they have the least feature and characteristic prominence of any creatures that God has made. With no playfulness, as silent as a fish, inactive, Bunny's life passes between a torpid half-slumber, and the nibbling of clover-tops, lettuce, plantain-leaves, pig-weed, and crumbs of bread. Sometimes, indeed, he is seized with a little impulse of friskiness; but it does not appear to be sportive, but nervous. Bunny has a singular countenance—like somebody's I have seen, but whose I forget. It is rather imposing and aristocratic, on a cursory glance, but examining it more closely, it is found to be laughably vague. Julian pays him very little attention now, and leaves me to take the whole labor of gathering leaves for him; else the poor little beast would be likely to starve. I am strongly tempted of the Evil One to murder him privately; and I wish with all my heart that Mrs. Peters would drown him.

Julian had a great resource, to-day, in my jack-knife, which, being fortunately as dull as a hoe, I have given him to whittle with. So he made what he called a boat; and has declared his purpose to make a tooth-pick for his mother, himself, Una, and me. He covered the floor of the boudoir with chips, twice over, and finds such inexhaustible amusement that I think it would be cheaply bought with the loss of one or two of his fingers.

At about half past six, I put him to bed, and walked to the post-office, where I found a letter from Mrs. Mann to Phoebe. I made no stay, and reached home, through a shower, at about eight. Went to bed without any supper—having nothing to eat but half-baked, sour bread.

TUESDAY, JULY 29TH, [1851].

Got up at six;—a cool, breezy morning, with sunshine glimpsing through sullen clouds, which seemed to hang low, and rest on the ridges of the hills that border our valley. I bathed, and then called Julian, who, by the by, was awake and summoning me, sometime before I was ready to receive him. He went with me for the milk, and frisked and capered along the road in a way that proved him to be in good physical condition. After breakfast, he immediately demanded the jack-knife, and proceeded to manufacture the tooth-picks. When the dew was off, we went out to the barn, and thence to the garden; and, in one way or another, half got through the forenoon until half-past ten—which is the present time of day.

Afterwards, he betook himself to playing bat and ball with huge racket and uproar about the room, felicitating himself continually on the license of making what noise he pleased, in the absence of baby. He enjoys this freedom so greatly, that I do not mean to restrain him, whatever noise he makes.

Then we took Bunny out into the open air, and put him down on the grass. Bunny appears to most advantage out of doors. His most interesting trait is the apprehensiveness of his nature; it is as quick, and as continually in movement, as an aspen leaf. The least noise startles him; and you may see his emotion in the movement of his ears; he starts, and scrambles into his little house, but, in a moment, peeps forth again, and begins nibbling the grass and weeds;—again to be startled, and as quickly re-assured. Sometimes he sets out on a nimble little run, for no reason, but just as a dry leaf is blown along by a puff of wind. I do not think that these fears are any considerable torment to Bunny; it is his nature to live in the midst of them, and to intermingle them, as a sort of piquant sauce, with every morsel he eats. It is what redeems his life from dulness and stagnation. Bunny appears to be uneasy in broad and open sunshine; it is his impulse to seek shadow—the shadow of a tuft of bushes, or Julian's shadow, or mine. He seemed to think himself in rather too much peril, so important a personage as he is, in the breadth of the yard, and took various opportunities to creep into Julian's lap. At last, the north-west breeze being cool to-day—too cool for me, especially when one of the thousand watery clouds intercepted the sun—we all three came in. This is a horrible, most hor-ri-ble climate; one knows not, for ten minutes together, whether he is too cool or too warm; but he is always one or the other; and the constant result is a miserable disturbance of the system. I detest it! I detest it!! I de-test it!!! I hate Berkshire with my whole soul, and would joyfully see its mountains laid flat. Luther and old Mr. Barnes speak as if this weather were something unusual. It may be so; but I rather conceive that a variable state of the atmosphere, in summer time, is incident to a country of hills, and always to be expected. At any rate, be it recorded that here, where I hoped for perfect health, I have for the first time been made sensible that I cannot with impunity encounter Nature in all her moods.

Since we came in, Julian has again betaken himself to that blessed jackknife, and is now "chipping and sharpening," as he calls it, and hammering, and talking to himself about his plans and performances, with great content.

After dinner (roast lamb for me, and boiled rice for Julian) we walked down to the lake. On our way, we waged war with thistles, which represented many-headed dragons and hydras, and on tall mulleins, which passed for giants. One of these latter offered such sturdy resistance that my stick was broken in the encounter; and so I cut it off of a length suitable to Julian;—whereupon he expressed

8

an odd entanglement of sorrow for my loss and joy at his own gain. Arriving at the lake, he dug most persistingly for worms, in order to catch a fish; but could find none. Then we threw innumerable stones into the water, for the pleasure of seeing the splash; also, I built a boat, with a scrap of newspaper for a sail, and sent it out on a voyage; and we could see the gleam of its sail, long afterwards, far away over the lake. It was a most beautiful afternoon— autumnal in its character—with a bright, warm, genial sunshine, but coolness in the air; so that, though it was rather beyond comfort to sit in the sun, I felt compelled to return to it after a brief experience of the shade. The heavy masses of cloud, lumbering about the sky, threw deep black shadows on the sunny hill-sides; so that the contrast between the heat and coolness of the day was thus visibly expressed. The atmosphere was particularly transparent, as if all the haze was collected into these dense clouds. Distant objects appeared with great distinctness; and the Taconic range of hills was a dark blue substance, with its protuberances and inequalities apparent—not cloud-like, as it often is. The sun smiled with mellow breadth across the rippling lake—rippling with the northwestern breeze.

On our way home, we renewed our warfare with the thistles; and they suffered terribly in the combat. Julian has a real spirit of battle in him, and puts his soul into his blows. Immediately after our return, he called for the jack-knife, and now keeps pestering me to look at the feats which he performs with it. Blessed be the man who invented jack-knives.

Next we went out and gathered some currents. He babbles constantly, throughout all these various doings, and often says odd things, which I either forget, or cannot possibly grasp them so as to write them down. Among other things, during the current gathering, he speculated about rainbows, and asked why they were not called sun-bows, or sun-rainbows; and said that he supposed their bow-strings were made of cobwebs; which was the reason why they could not be seen. Some of the time, I hear him repeating poetry, with good emphasis and intonation. He is never out of temper or out of spirits, and is certainly as happy as the day is long. He is happy enough by himself; and when I sympathize or partake in his play, it is almost too much; and he nearly explodes with laughter and delight.

Little Marshall Butler has just been in to inquire whether "the bird" has come yet. I am afraid we shall be favored with visits every day till it comes. I do wish the original parrot had been given him, whatever its defects; for I have seldom suffered more from the presence of any individual than from that of this odious little urchin. Julian took no more notice of him than if he had not been present; but went on with his talk and occupations, displaying an equanimity which I could not but envy. He absolutely ignores him; no practised man of the world could do it better, or half so well. After prying about the room, and examining the playthings, Marshall took himself off.

It was towards seven o'clock when I put him to bed; nor need I hesitate to say that I was glad to get rid of him—it being my first relief from his society during the whole day. This may be too much of a good thing.

At about eight, Mrs. Tappan came in, bringing three newspapers and the first volume of Pendennis. She seemed in very pleasant mood. I read the papers till ten, and then to bed.

WEDNESDAY, JULY 30TH, [1851].

Got up not much before seven. A chill and lowery morning, with, I think, a south-east wind, threatening rain. Julian lounges about, lies on the floor, and seems in some degree responsive to the weather. I trust we are not going to be visited with a long storm.

The day is so unpropitious that we have taken no

forenoon walk; but only idle about the barn and garden. Bunny has grown quite familiar, and comes hopping to meet us, whenever we enter the room, and stands on his hind legs, to see whether we have anything for him. Julian has changed his name (which was Spring) to Hindlegs. One finds himself getting rather attached to this gentle little beast, especially when he shows confidence, and makes himself at home. It is rather troublesome, however, to find him food; for he seems to want to eat almost constantly, yet does not like his grass or leaves, unless they are entirely fresh. Bread he nibbles a little, but soon quits it. I have just got him some green oats from Mr. Tappan's field. Of all eatables, he seems to like Julian's shoes better than anything; and indulges himself with a taste of them on all possible occasions.

At four o'clock, I dressed him up; and we set out for the village; he frisking and capering like a little goat, and gathering flowers like a child of paradise. The flowers had not the least beauty in them, except what his eyes made by looking at them; nevertheless, he thought them the loveliest in the world. We met a carriage with three or four young ladies, all whom were evidently smitten by his potent charms. Indeed, he seldom passes anything with a petticoat, without carrying away her heart. It is very odd; for I see no such wonderful magic in the young gentleman.

Arriving at the Post Office, I found—greatly to my disappointment; for indeed I had not conceived the possibility—no letter from Phoebe, nor anything else for myself; nothing but a letter and paper for Mr. Tappan. So I put in a letter for Pike, which I wrote some days ago, and had forgotten to send, and a brief letter for Phoebe, which I wrote to-day—and we immediately set out on our return. Ascending the hill, on this side of Mr. Birch's, we met a wagon, in which sat Mr. James, his wife, and daughter, who had just left their cards at our house. Here ensued a talk, quite pleasant and friendly. He is certainly an excellent man, and his wife is a plain, good, friendly, kind-hearted woman, and the daughter a nice girl;—nevertheless, Julian thought Mr. James rather tedious, and said that he did not like his talk at all. In fact, the poor little urchin was tired to death with standing. Mr. James spoke of the House of the Seven Gables, and of Twice-told Tales, and thence branched off upon English literature generally.

Reaching home, we found Julian's supper ready; and he has eaten it, and appears quite ready for bed—whither I shall now (at half past six) consign him.

I read Pendennis during the evening, and concluded the day with a bowl of egg-nog.

THURSDAY, JULY 31ST, [1851].

———

At about six o'clock, I looked over the edge of my bed, and saw that Julian was awake, peeping sideways at me out of his eyes, with a subdued laugh in them. So we got up; and first I bathed him, and then myself; and afterwards I proposed to curl his hair. I forgot to say that I attempted the same thing, the morning before last, and succeeded miraculously ill; indeed, it was such a failure, that the old boy burst into a laugh at the first hint of repeating the attempt. However, I persisted, and screwed his hair round a stick, till I almost screwed it out of his head; he all the time squealing and laughing, between pain and merriment. He endeavored to tell me how his mother proceeded; but his instructions were not very clear, and only entangled the business so much the more. But, now that his hair is dry, it does not look so badly as might have been expected.

After thus operating on his wig, we went for the milk. It was another cloudy and lowery morning, with a cloud (which looked as full of moisture as a wet sponge) lying all along the ridge of the western hill; beneath which the wooded hill-side looked black, grim, and desolate. Monument Mountain, too, had a cloud on its back; but the sunshine gleamed along its sides, and made it quite a cheerful object; and being in the centre of the scene, it cheered up the whole picture, like a cheery heart. Even its forests, as contrasted with the woods on the other hills, had a light on them; and the cleared tracts seemed doubly sunny, and a field of rye, just at its base, shone out with yellow radiance, and quite illuminated the landscape. As we walked along, the little man munched a bread-cake, and talked about the "jew" (as he pronounced it) on the grass, and said that he supposed fairies had been pouring it on the grass and flowers, out of their little pitchers. Then he pestered me to tell him on which side of the road I thought the dewy grass looked prettiest. Thus, with all the time a babble at my side, as if a brook were running along the way, we reached Luther's house; and old Atropos took the pail, with a grim smile, and gave it back with two quarts of milk.

The weather being chill, and the sun not constant or powerful enough to dry off the dew, we spent the greater part of the forenoon within doors. The old gentleman, as usual, bothered me with innumerable questions, and continual references as to all his occupations.

After dinner, we took a walk to the lake. As we drew near the bank, we saw a boat a little off the shore; and another approached the strand, and its crew landed, just afterwards. They were three men, of a loaferish aspect. They asked me whether there was any good water near at hand; then they strolled inland, to view the country, as is the custom of voyagers on setting foot in foreign parts. Hereupon, Julian went to their boat, which he viewed with great interest, and gave a great exclamation on discovering some fish in it. They were only a few bream and pouts. The little man wanted me to get into the boat and sail off with him; and he could hardly be got away from the spot. I made him a shingle skiff, and launched it, and it went away westward—the wind being east to-day. Then we made our way along the tangled lake-shore, and sitting down, he threw in bits of moss, and called them islands—floating green islands—and said that there were trees, and farms, and men, upon them. By and by, against his remonstrances, I insisted upon going home. He picked up a club, and began over again the old warfare with the thistles—which we called hydras, chimaeras, dragons, and Gorgons. Thus we fought our way homeward; and so has passed the day, until now at twenty minutes past four.

In the earlier part of the summer, I thought that the landscape would suffer by the change from pure and rich verdure, after the pastures should turn yellow, and the fields be mowed. But I now think the change an improvement. The contrast between the faded green, and, here and there, the almost brown and dusky fields, as compared with the deep green of the woods, is very picturesque, on the hill-sides.

Before supper, Mrs. Tappan came in, with two or three volumes of Fourier's works, which I wished to borrow, with a view to my next Romance. She proposed that Julian should come over and see Ellen tomorrow; to which I not unwillingly gave my assent; and the old gentleman, too, seemed pleased with the prospect. He has now had his supper, and is forthwith to be put to bed. Mrs. Peter's, whose husband is sick or unwell (probably drunk,) is going home to-night, and will return in the morning. And now Julian is in bed, and I have gathered and crushed some currents, and have given Bunny his supper of lettuce, which he seems to like better than anything else; though nothing in the vegetable line comes amiss to him. He ate a leaf of mint to-day, seemingly with great relish. It makes me smile to see how he invariably comes galloping to meet me, whenever I open the door, making sure that there is something in store for him, and smelling eagerly to find out what it is. He eats enormously, and, I think, has grown considerably broader than when he came hither. The mystery that broods about him—the lack of any method of communicating with this voiceless creature—heightens the interest. Then he is naturally so full of little alarms, that it is pleasant to find him free of these, as to Julian and myself.

FRIDAY, AUGUST 1ST, [1851].

———

This was another chill and sulky day; so cool that I put a knit-jacket on Julian, when we went for the milk. There was a general conclave of cloud overhead, but interspersed with blue, and then partial gleams of watery sunshine. Monument Mountain was in shadow, this morning, and the western ridge had the sun on it. The atmosphere was particularly clear; insomuch that I do not recollect ever seeing Taconic bulge so prominently forth from its outline as it did now. It looked but a little further off than the Monument.

Bruin ran along with us, much to Julian's delight; but on our return, the dog began to caper and frisk somewhat obstreperously—whereupon the old gentleman was seized with congenital dread of the canine cur, and burst out crying.

It was so cheerless out of doors, that we spent the morning within. I was occupied with two letters (excruciatingly short ones) from Phoebe, and with papers, which Mrs. Peters had brought from the post-office. At about eleven, came Deborah and little Ellen, to take Julian to Highwood; so his majesty departed, and I saw nothing more of him till after dinner. I packed up and sent off Phoebe's sculpturing tools, which Mrs. Mann wants for

some purpose or other. I trust Phoebe will not be persuaded among all her other cares and annoyances, to
undertake any alteration or modification of his bust. If
this had occurred to me sooner, I certainly should not
have sent the tools.

We had, to-day, the first string beans of the season; the
earliest product of our garden, indeed, except currants
and lettuce. At three o'clock, came Julian home. He said
that he had tomatoes, beans, and asparagus, for dinner,
and that he liked them very much, and had had a good
time. I dressed him and myself for a walk to the village,
and we set out at four. The mail not being in, at our
arrival, we went to Mr. Farley's office (where we saw him
and Mr. Sedgwick) and afterwards to Mr. Farley's house, or
rather to his hen-coop, to see his splendid rooster and
chickens. I gave Mr. Sedgwick to understand, by the by,
that we should take Mrs. Kemble's house in the autumn.
Returning to the Post office, I got Mr. Tappan's mail and
my own, and proceeded homeward, but clambered over
the fence and sat down in Love Grove, to read the papers.
While thus engaged, a cavalier on horseback came along
the road, and saluted me in Spanish; to which I replied by
touching my hat, and went on with the newspaper. But
the cavalier renewing his salutation, I regarded him more
attentively, and saw that it was Herman Melville! So,
hereupon, Julian and I hastened to the road, where ensued

a greeting, and we all went homeward together, talking as we went. Soon, Mr. Melville alighted, and put Julian into the saddle; and the little man was highly pleased, and sat on the horse with the freedom and fearlessness of an old equestrian, and had a ride of at least a mile homeward.

I asked Mrs. Peters to make some tea for Herman Melville; and so she did, and he drank a cup, but was afraid to drink much, because it would keep him awake. After supper, I put Julian to bed; and Melville and I had a talk about time and eternity, things of this world and of the next, and books, and publishers, and all possible and impossible matters, that lasted pretty deep into the night; and if truth must be told, we smoked cigars even within the sacred precincts of the sitting-room. At last, he arose, and saddled his horse (whom we had put into the barn) and rode off for his own domicile; and I hastened to make the most of what little sleeping-time remained for me.

SATURDAY, AUGUST 2D, [1851].

In the morning, we got up at about $1/2$ past six, and, Julian being bathed, and also myself, and Julian's wool duly frizzled, we set out for the milk. For the first time since some immemorial date, it was really a pleasant morning; not a cloud to be seen, except a few white and bright streaks, far off to the southward. Monument Mountain, however, had a fleece of sun-brightened mist, entirely covering it except its western summit, which emerged. There were also mists along the western side, hovering on the tree-tops, and portions of the same mist had flitted upwards, and become real clouds in the sky. These vapors were rapidly passing away; and by the time we had done our errand, and returned, they had wholly disappeared.

I forgot to say, in the record of last night, that Herman Melville invited me to bring Julian and spend several days at his house, next week, when E. A. Duyckinck and his brother are to be there. I accepted for at least one night; and so Melville is to come for us.

At ten o'clock, I sent Julian over to Highwood, with Bunny, whom he is going to offer as a present to Ellen. The truth is, our house is too small, and we have not proper accommodations for the excellent Bunny, for whom I have a great regard, but whose habits do not exactly fit him to be a constant occupant of the sitting room. Our straw-carpet was beginning to suffer seriously from some of his proceedings. At Highwood, they can give him a room to himself, if they like—or, in short, do what they please with him. I really liked Bunny, who has very pleasant little ways, and a character well worth observing. He had grown perfectly familiar with us, and seemed to show a fondness for our society, and would always sit himself near us, and was attentive to all our motions. He has, I think, a great deal of curiosity, and an investigating disposition, and is very observant of what is going on around him. I do not know any other beast, and few human beings, who, always present, and thrusting his little paw into all the business of the day, could at the same time be so perfectly unobtrusive. I cannot but regret his departure, both for our sakes and his own; for I am afraid Ellen will squeeze and otherwise torment him, and that he will find nobody at Highwood so attentive to his habits as I was. What a pity that he could not have put himself under some restraint and rule, as to certain matters. Julian, too, seemed half-sorry to part with Bunny, but was so pleased with the idea of giving him to Ellen that he made no objection. He has not yet returned to say how the offering was accepted.

¼ of eleven, Julian has come back, and reports that they did not thank him for Bunny, and that Ellen began to squeeze him very hard, the first minute. He saw Deborah, and Caroline, and Ellen. They did not understand, at first, that Bunny was to remain there; and when Julian was coming away, they asked him if he was going to leave Bunny. "Why," said the little man, "he is to be Ellen's own!"—whereat they said nothing. He says, however, that they seemed to be glad to have it. Poor Bunny, I am afraid, is doomed to be a sufferer for the rest of his life. Ellen, according to Julian's account, took the poor little fellow up by his fur, and by his hind-leg, keeping him dangling in the air, and committed various other outrages. Perhaps I had better have drowned him. Possibly I may yet have a chance to do so; for I should not wonder if they were to send him back. Julian says he had a great mind to snatch him away and run home.

Before dinner, we took a walk to the lake, where we found a boat drawn up on the shore; and if it had not been fastened to the root of a tree, and locked, I think we should have taken a trip to foreign parts. The little man got into the boat, and enjoyed himself greatly; especially when he discovered some little old fish, evidently of some days' continuance, in the bottom of the boat.

After dinner came Mr. Farley, as he had partly given me to expect, when I saw him yesterday. He came with the purpose of trying to catch some fish; so all three of us went down to the lake. Julian was quite in ecstacy. There is no use trying to keep him from becoming a fisherman; there is the genuine instinct in him; and sooner or later, it will gratify itself. Neither do I perceive any reason why it should not; it is as harmless a propensity as he could have. However, there was nothing in our luck, this afternoon, to make him enamored of the pursuit. We caught only a few bream and perch, each of which the old gentleman immediately took up by the tail, surveying it with most delighted interest, and frisking all the while as if in sympathy with the frisky movements of the poor fish. After a while, Mr. Farley and I became tired, and we set out for home. The afternoon was as perfect as could be, as to beauty and comfort; just warm enough; nothing to be added or taken away. He did not stay to tea, but went home, taking Herman Melville's "White Jacket" with him.

I put Julian to bed at seven, or thereabouts, and went out to pick some currants. While thus engaged, Mrs. Tappan passed by the edge of the garden, towards the lower barn; and I asked her whether Julian made his offering of the rabbit to Ellen, with due grace. She laughed, and said that he did, but said that they found Bunny quite troublesome, and that Ellen maltreated him, and that the dog was always trying to get him—and, in short, Bunny turned out not to be a desirable acquisition. She spoke of giving him to little Marshall Butler, and suggested, moreover (in reply to something that I said about putting him out of existence) that he might be turned out into the woods, to shift for himself. There is something characteristic in this idea; it shows the sort of sensitiveness, that finds the pain and misery of other people disagreeable, just as it would a bad scent, but is perfectly at ease when once they are removed from her sphere. I suppose she would not for the world have killed Bunny, although she would have exposed him to the certainty of lingering starvation, without scruple or remorse. Seeing nothing else to be done, I proposed to take Bunny back, and she promised to bring him tomorrow.

Mrs. Peters went home immediately after supper. I read Pendennis during the evening, ate about a quart of crushed currants, and went to bed at ten.

SUNDAY, AUGUST 3D, [1851].

The little man woke me with his exclamation between two and three o'clock; and I found him, wonderful to say, in a perfectly soppy state. There had been a deluge in his bed, and nowhere else. So I was forced to go down stairs and find him a clean nightgown, and make what other arrangements I could for his comfort. It is almost an unprecedented accident with him.

It was long before I fell asleep again; and then I did not awake till half past six, when he appeared to have been awake a considerable time. I bathed him and myself; as usual, made a fire in the kitchen, and went for the milk. It was a perfect morning, with broad and bright sunshine, and, I believe, not a single cloud over the whole sky; unless it were a few mist-wreaths here and there on the distant hill sides. The lake was as smooth as glass, and gave motionless reflections of the woods and hills. This glassy surface is the best aspect of so small a sheet of water. At Luther Butler's, we found his father-in-law, old Mr. Barnes, cutting a young man's hair. The patient was seated in a chair at the kitchen-door; and the old fellow seemed to perform the operation with a good deal of skill, and had made a pretty even surface all over his head, leaving the hair about an inch long.

I told Julian that I was going to send him to get Bunny after breakfast. The little man's phiz quite glowed with delight, but yet he seemed confused. "Why, father," said he, "you see I left Bunny there to be Ellen's own; so I can't take him, unless they should send him back." I quieted his scruples, by telling him what Mrs. Tappan had said; and he immediately became very desirous to go and get Bunny. At about nine o'clock, I let him go; and in half an hour or so, he came back with Bunny, in his little house. Poor Bunny seemed to have lost a good deal of his confidence in human nature, and kept himself as close as he could in a corner of the box, and made no response to my advances, nor would take a lettuce-leaf which I offered him. I rather think he has lived in great torment during his absence. Julian says it was a great while before he could come away with him, on account of Bruin; so desirous was that naughty dog to get poor little Bunny.

I read Pendennis till twelve, while the old boy amused himself hither and thither; then, seeing him down in the valley, I went and lay under an apple-tree [   ]. Julian climbed up into the tree, and sat astride of a branch. His round merry face appeared among the green leaves, and a continual stream of babble came dripping down upon me, like a summer shower. He said how he should like to live always in the tree, and make a nest of leaves. Then he wanted to be a bird, so that he might fly far away; and he would go to a deep hole, and bring me back a bag of gold; and he would fly to West Newton, and bring home mamma on his back; and he would fly to the Post Office for letters, and he would get beans, and squashes, and potatoes. After a while, I took him down from the tree; and removing a little way from the spot, we chanced upon a remarkable echo. It repeated every word of his clear little voice, at his usual elevation of talk; and when either of us called loudly, we could hear as many as three or four repetitions—the last coming apparently from far away beyond the woods, with a strange, fantastic similitude to the original voice, as if beings somewhat like ourselves were shouting in the invisible distance. Julian called

"Mamma," "Una," and many other words; then he shouted his own name, and when the sound came back upon us, he said that mamma was calling him. What a strange, weird thing is an echo, to be sure!

At two o'clock the whole family had dinner; Julian an end of bread, myself a custard-pie, and Bunny some nibblings of the crust. The little man and I then walked down to the lake. The crusade against the thistles still continues; and the mulleins likewise come in for their share of the blows. After loitering awhile on the shore of the lake, we came homeward through Mr. Wilcox's field and through his tall pine-wood. I lay on my back, looking upward through the branches of the trees, while Julian spent nearly a quarter of an hour, I should think, beating down a single great mullein-stalk. He certainly does evince a persevering purpose, sometimes. We strolled through the wood among the tall pillars of those primaeval pines, and thence home along the margin of a swamp, in which I gathered a sheaf of cat-tails. This brings the history up to the present time, within a few minutes of five o'clock.

Either I have less patience to-day than ordinary, or the little man makes larger demands upon it; but it really does seem as if he had baited me with more questions, references, and observations, than mortal father ought to be expected to endure. He does put me almost beside my propriety; never quitting me, and continually thrusting in his word between the clauses of every sentence of all my reading, and smashing every attempt at reflection into a thousand fragments.

I put him to bed at seven; gathered and crushed some currants; took a meditative walk to-and-fro, behind the house, looking out on the lake and hills; ate the currants; pored over a paper (having finished the first volume of Pendennis,) and went to bed before ten.

MONDAY, AUGUST 4TH, [1851].

We got up at about half past six; and before the bathing was over Mrs. Peters arrived. Going for the milk, the sun shone warm, but not bright, through a thin cloudiness that was diffused over the whole sky. The little man seemed to be sprightly and in good condition, although he had tumbled about, during the night, to a degree that often woke me up. After breakfast, I gathered a tray full of string beans from my garden, and Julian a tin pailfull from his own individual domain.

The little man has been speculating about his mother's

age, and says she is twenty years old. "So very small," he exclaims, "and twenty years old!"

The weather grew very chill, as the day advanced, with the wind from the eastward. Oh, for an east-wind with a breath of the salt sea in it. Of course, this infernal atmosphere has given me a cold; and I have sat shivering all day, with an utter disinclination to move. All day, I mean, until somewhat past four, when Julian and I set out for the village. The little man has kept up his spirits, and has hammered and pounded at some carpenter work or other, greatly to the discomfort of my head; although I fell into a half drowse in the midst of it. On our road to the village, he trotted off like a young colt, on his short, but unweariable legs. Reaching the office, we found no letter; the eastern mail had somehow or other failed to arrive—a miserable mischance. After stepping into the court-house to see Mr. Farley, and sitting awhile in his office, we turned our faces homeward; the old gentleman pestering me sorely to get him an orange—which, however, I could not have done, without a long walk to the other end of the village. He seemed just as active and frisky as ever, on our homeward road; while I was grim, gloomy, and utterly without elasticity. I turned up the avenue to Highwood, with a letter and paper for Willy Barney; and finding the study-window open, I stept in and took the Home Journal, which I looked over, in a chair, under the porch.

I put Julian to bed at seven, and then wrapt myself in my wadded gown, and sat in the boudoir;—took some Nux vomica, and went to bed before ten.

TUESDAY, AUGUST 5TH, [1851].

I slept pretty well, and so did the old gentleman; although he awoke me once with his tumblings and tossings. We got up, as usual, at half past six; my cold being apparently on the mending hand. The weather, as we found on going for the milk, was rather less chill than yesterday; but there were leaden clouds over the whole sky, here and there resting on the ridges of the hills. No wind at all; the lake perfectly smooth. Coming home from Luther's, the little man lingered behind to gather some flowers, and then setting out to run, he came down with a terrible tumble.

It now lacks a quarter of eleven o'clock. The only remarkable event, thus far, has been a visit. I was sitting in the boudoir, when a knock came to the front-door; and Mrs. Peters said that a lady wished to see me; so I went up stairs on tiptoe, and made myself as presentable as I could, at short notice, and came down to the drawing-room. The visiter was a lady, rather young, and quite comely, with pleasant and intelligent eyes, in a pretty Quaker dress. She offered me her hand, and spoke with much simplicity, but yet in a ladylike way, of her interest in my works, and her not being able to resist a desire to see me, on finding herself in my vicinity. I asked her into the sitting-room, to enjoy our back view; and we talked of the scenery, and of various persons and matters. Lowell, Whittier, Mr. James, and Herman Melville, were more or less discussed; she seemed to be a particular friend of Whittier, and had heard of his calling on me, two or three years ago. Her manners were very agreeable indeed; the Quaker simplicity, and the little touch of Quaker phraseology, gave piquancy to her refinement and air of society. She had a pleasant smile, and eyes that readily responded to one's thought; so that it was not difficult to talk with her;—a singular, but yet a gentle freedom in expressing her own opinions;—an entire absence of affectation. These were the traits that impressed me; and, on the whole, it was the only pleasant visit I ever experienced, in my capacity as author. She did not bore me with laudations of my own writings, but merely said that there are some authors with whom we felt ourselves privileged to be acquainted, by the nature of our sympathy with their writings—or something to that effect, &c &c &c.

All this time, Julian was clambering into my lap, and acting otherwise like a great, aukward, overgrown baby. He had on a knit-jacket, which I had thought it prudent to endue him with, in the morning, on account of the east-wind. This, however, I took off, in the lady's presence. I had brushed and frizzled his hair, after breakfast; but it only looked the worse for my pains. She smiled on him, and praised his healthy aspect, and inquired whether he looked like his mother—observing that he had no resemblance to myself. Finally, she rose to depart, and I ushered her to the gate, where, as she took leave, she told me her name—"Elizabeth Lloyd"—and bidding me "Farewell!", she went on her way, and I saw her no more. She had not ridden hither, but was on a walk. She resides in Philadelphia. Julian allowed her to kiss him.

I have read Fourier to-day, when I have read anything. After dinner, we set out on a walk down to the lake. The weather is still uncertain, threatening rain all the time, and never fulfilling its threat. It might more properly be called a promise, now, than a threat; for it is an exceedingly dry time indeed. There are five or six feet more of margin to the lake, than I ever saw before; and the brook is quite dry, along a great part of its channel. The effect of the drought is visible in the foliage of the woods; it has shrunken within a few days, so that the shade which it casts is not so dense as before. This lack of moisture may

33

be one reason that withered and yellow leaves, and even branches, begin to be seen. But many autumnal characteristics may now be detected; the yellow flowers, the yellow hue of grain fields, the no longer juicy, but crispy herbage—everything tells the story of a past climax. And when did it pass? I am sure I don't know.

On our way home Julian was stung in the leg by a wasp, and squealed outrageously. This was in getting over the fence by Mr. Tappan's oat-field. He seemed quite in an agony, at first, but was so far recovered, before we reached the house, that he asked for a piece of bread and some water, more earnestly than a cure for the bite. I first bathed his leg in arnica, and then fed him. All this has brought us to a quarter past five. He continues to pester me with his inquisitions. For instance, just now, while he is whittling with my jack-knife. "Father, if you had bought all the jack-knives at the shop, what would you do for another, when you broke them all?" "I would go somewhere else," say I. But there is no stumping him so. "If you had bought all the jack-knives in the world, what would you do?" And here my patience gives way, and I entreat him not to trouble me with any more foolish questions. I really think it would do him good to spank him, apropos to this habit.

I put him to bed between six and seven; and, my cold being not quite well, went to bed myself at nine.

WEDNESDAY, AUGUST 6TH, [1851].

We got up about the usual time. The little man's leg and foot were swollen and inflamed, in consequence of the wasp-bite of yesterday; and he complained of pain when the part was touched, though otherwise it seemed to be comfortable enough. I gave him two globules of Aconite; and advised him not to go with me for the milk; but he insisted, and got along without any inconvenience. It was a clear, mild morning, with some clouds, but a singularly transparent atmosphere. We got some butter at Luther's; and being myself burthened with the milk, I gave it to the old gentleman to carry. He remonstrated, in a sharp, quick, high voice, sounding very much like the chattering of an angry squirrel; but when I reasoned with him, and pointed out the impropriety of my carrying two burthens, while he had none, he yielded at once; and refused to let me take the butter when I thought he had carried it far enough.

After breakfast, we gathered some summer squashes, the first our garden has produced. Then I frizzled his wig; an art in which I do not perceive that I make any improvement. It was before ten, I think, when we set forth on a walk to the lake; it being a beautiful forenoon, with warmth in the sun, and coolness in the breaths of

wind. At the lake, the little man provided himself with
an old dry branch of a tree, to the end of which he fastened a straw, and began to fish, with a faith that it was
really piteous to behold. Afterwards, we went through
the green, glimmering wood to the beach near the Stock-
bridge road, where we both amused ourselves for sometime setting sticks and chips afloat. For my part, I felt
very inactive with this lazy, benumbing cold, which
hangs on longer than usual. It made me no fit playmate
for this frisky little monster. It was after twelve when we
got home.

After dinner, we went out to the barn, and refreshed
ourselves among the new hay; and when we came in, I
found two letters—one from Phoebe, giving a brief sum-
mary of her wearinesses; the other from Pike, concern-
ing a plan for a seashore residence. Having previously
intended to go to the village, this afternoon, we set out, at
a little past four. It was a hot sun, with now and then a
puff of cool breeze; the same poisonous weather that we
have had so much of, this summer; but the breeze was
enjoyable, nevertheless. I found nothing at the office, save
the Museum, and a letter from an autograph-collector.
I bought [jam], [...] as my only comfort. Julian was
remarkably uneasy in the village; insomuch that I came
away without purchasing some loaf-sugar, which we have
wanted ever so long. He was so restless in his movements

that I suspected him to be, in his technical phrase, "uncomfortable"; but he positively denied it. We stopt at Love-Grove; and there again I made inquisition as to this point; but he still said no. He was so restless, however, that I advised him to go home before me, and he accordingly started at a great pace. I came up with him, on the ascent of the hill, on this side of Mr. Butler's. I heard him squealing, while I was some distance behind; and approaching nearer, I saw that he walked wide between the legs. Poor little man! His drawers were all a-sop. It is a positive cruelty to the child not to put him into such a dress that he may have nature's freedom, at any moment. Boys do not like to tell their necessities, especially when they are abnormally frequent as his appear to be to-day.

I put him to bed at about seven. It is now between eight and nine. In the dusk of the evening, just now, came Mrs. Tappan to borrow some eggs (I lent her seven) and to ask if I mean to write again to Sophia, before her return. In that case, she wishes her to get ten pounds of ground rice.

I looked over a newspaper, during the evening, and to bed before ten.

THURSDAY, AUGUST 7TH, [1851].

We got up rather later than usual, this morning; not till seven o'clock by our time-piece, which, however, is twenty minutes faster than the village clock. A still, warm morning, with the sun already shining fervently, though muffled by here and there a cloud. We went on our customary milky way. The aspect of the hills was varied from what it has been for some time past, by a sunny haze that involved distant objects in a still greater remoteness. It was a lazy morning. I myself felt it particularly so; and the little man acknowledged the same influence by the absence of somewhat of his ordinary friskiness; but so did not two or three squirrels whom we saw scampering along on the tops of the fences. Julian talked about poison-flowers, with which, according to him, the roadside is bordered, and which are not to be touched with the naked hand.

After breakfast, we gathered some beans; then I frizzled his wool. It is observable, that his hair does not begin to present a respectable appearance until the day after I have been at work upon it; so that, every morning, I regularly spoil my own handiwork of the day before. His patience under the operation is most exemplary.

In the course of the forenoon, it became showery, so

that we could make no excursions farther than to the shed and barn. Mr. Waldo, who had one of his little girls with him in the field, brought her hither for a few minutes. She is quite a pretty child, about three years old, with large dark eyes, and a queer little merry face. Julian kept himself in reserve, and offered few or no attentions, except to run and get Bunny, at my suggestion. He is getting to be a boy, in this respect; that is to say, a little monster of stupid good manners. She was much tickled with Bunny, whom she took to be a kind of little cat; and I was not without hopes of disposing of this valuable animal to Mr. Waldo, for his daughter's behoof;—but he did not offer to take Bunny. I talked with him on Fourierism and kindred subjects, and he seems to be a man of thought and intelligence. He said that Cornelius was going to the village today; and I gave him a letter which I had written to Phoebe, to be put in the Post Office—which I rather regret, as I shall have no certitude of its being mailed. So I must write another before Saturday.

It has continued quite showery, through the afternoon. Just now, there was a very picturesque scene, if I could but paint it in words. Across our valley, from east to west, there was a heavy canopy of clouds, almost resting on the hills on either side. It did not extend southward so far as Monument Mountain, which lay in sunshine, and with a sunny cloud midway on its bosom; and from the midst of our storm, beneath our black roof of clouds, we looked out upon this bright scene, where the people were enjoying beautiful weather. The clouds hung so low over us, that it was like being in a tent, the entrance of which was drawn up, permitting us to see the sunny landscape. This lasted for several minutes; but at last the shower stretched southward, and quite snatched away Monument Mountain, and made it invisible; although now it is mistily re-appearing. I suppose such a [. . .] [of the gaps] of the weather.

Julian has got rid of the afternoon in a miscellaneous way; making a whip, and a bow and arrow, and playing jack-straws with himself for an antagonist. It was less than an hour, I think, after dinner, when he began to teaze for something to eat; although he dined abundantly on rice and string-beans. I allowed him a slice of bread in the middle of the afternoon; and an hour afterwards, he began to bellow at the full stretch of his lungs for more, and beat me terribly, because I refused it. He is really as strong as a little giant. He asked me just now—"What are sensible questions?"—I suppose with a view to asking me some.

After a most rampageous resistance, the old gentleman was put to bed at seven o'clock. I ought to mention that Mrs. Peters is quite attentive to him, in her grim way. To-day, for instance, we found two ribbons on his old straw hat, which must have been of her sewing on. She encourages no familiarity on his part, nor is he in the least drawn towards her, nor, on the other hand, does he exactly seem to stand in awe; but he recognizes that there is to be no communication beyond the inevitable—and, with that understanding, she awards him all substantial kindness.

To bed not long after nine.

FRIDAY, AUGUST 8TH, [1851].

———

It was not much later than six when we got up. A pleasant morning, with a warm sun, and clouds lumbering about, especially to the northward and eastward; the relics of yesterday's showeriness, and perhaps foreboding similar weather to-day. When we went for the milk, Mrs. Butler told me that she could not let us have any more butter, at present; so that we must have recourse to Highwood. Before breakfast, the little man heard a cat mewing; and on investigation, we found that the noise proceeded from the cistern. I removed a plank, and sure enough, there seemed to be a cat swimming for her life in it. Mrs. Peter's heard her, last night; and probably she had been there ten or twelve hours, paddling in that dismal hole. After many efforts to get her out, I at last let down a bucket, into which she made shift to scramble, and so I drew her out. The poor thing was almost exhausted, and could scarcely crawl; and no wonder, after such a night as she must have spent. We gave her some milk, of which she lapped a little. It was one of the kittens.

Early in the forenoon, came Deborah with Ellen, to see Julian and Bunny. Julian was quite silent. Between eleven and twelve, came Herman Melville, and the two Duyckincks, in a barouche and pair. Melville had spoken, when he was here, of bringing these two expected guests of his to call on me; and I intended, should it be anywise practicable, to ask them to stay to dinner; but we had nothing whatever in the house to-day. It passed well enough, however; for they proposed a ride and a pic-nic, to which I readily consented. In the first place, however, I produced our only remaining bottle of Mr. Mansfield's champaigne; after which we set out, taking Julian, of course. It was an admirable day; neither too cold nor too hot—with some little shadow of clouds, but no appearance of impending rain. We took the road over the mountain towards Hudson, and by and by came to a pleasant grove, where we alighted and arranged matters for our pic-nic.

After all, I suspect they had considered the possibility, if not probability, of my giving them a dinner; for the repast was neither splendid nor particularly abundant—

only some sandwiches and gingerbread. There was nothing whatever for Julian, except the gingerbread; for the bread, which encased the sandwiches, was buttered, and moreover had mustard on it. So I had to make the little man acquainted, for the first time in his life, with gingerbread; and he seemed to be greatly pleased until he had eaten a considerable quantity—when he began to discover that it was not quite the thing to make a meal of. However, his hunger was satisfied and no harm done; besides that there were a few nuts and raisins at the bottom of the basket, whereof he ate and was contented. He enjoyed the ride and the whole thing exceedingly, and behaved like a man experienced in pic-nics.

After a smoke under the trees, and talk about literature and other things, we set forth again, and resolved to go and visit the Shaker establishment at Hancock, which was but two or three miles off. I don't know what Julian expected to see—some strange sort of quadruped or other, I suppose—at any rate, the term "Shakers" was evidently a subject of great puzzlement with him; and probably he was a little disappointed when I pointed out an old man in a gown and a gray, broad-brimmed hat, as a Shaker. This old man was one of the fathers and rulers of the village; and under his guidance, we visited the principal dwelling-house in the village. It was a large brick edifice, with admirably convenient arrangements, and floors and walls of polished wood, and plaster as smooth as marble, and everything so neat that it was a pain and constraint to look at it; especially as it did not imply any real delicacy or moral purity in the occupants of the house. There were spit-boxes (bearing no appearance of ever being used, it is true) at equal distances up and down the long and broad entries. The sleeping apartments of the two sexes had an entry between them, on one side of which hung the hats of the men, on the other the bonnets of the women. In each chamber were two particularly narrow beds, hardly wide enough for one sleeper, but in each of which, the old elder told us, two people slept. There were no bathing or washing conveniences in the chambers; but in the entry there was a sink and wash-bowl, where all their attempts at purification were to be performed. The fact shows that all their miserable pretence of cleanliness and neatness is the thinnest superficiality; and that the Shakers are and must needs be a filthy set. And then their utter and systematic lack of privacy; their close junction of man with man, and supervision of one man over another—it is hateful and disgusting to think of; and the sooner the sect is extinct the better—a consummation which, I am happy to hear, is thought to be not a great many years distant.

In the great house, we saw an old woman—a round, fat, cheerful little old sister—and two girls, from nine to twelve years old; these looked at us and at Julian with great curiosity, though slily and with side glances. At the doors of other dwellings, we saw women sewing or otherwise at work; and there seemed to be a kind of comfort among them, but of no higher kind than is enjoyed by their beasts of burden. Also, the women looked pale, and none of the men had a jolly aspect. They are certainly the most singular and bedevilled set of people that ever existed in a civilized land; and one of these days, when their sect and system shall have passed away, a History of the Shakers will be a very curious book. All through this outlandish village went our little man hopping and dancing, in excellent spirits; nor had he been long there before he desired to confer with himself—neither was I unwilling that he should bestow such a mark of his consideration (being the one of which they were most worthy) on the system and establishment of these foolish Shakers.

I think it was about five o'clock when we left the village. Lenox was probably seven or eight miles distant; but we mistook the road, and went up hill and down, through unknown regions, over at least twice as much ground as there was any need. It was by far the most picturesque ride that I ever had in Berkshire. On one height, just before sunset, we had a view for miles and miles around, with the Kaatskills blue and far on the horizon. Then the road ran along the verge of a deep gulf—deep, deep, deep, and filled with foliage of trees that could not reach half way up to us; and on the other side of the chasm uprose a mountainous precipice. This continued for a good distance; and on the other side of the road there were occasional openings through the forest, that showed the low country at the base of the mountain. If I could find the way, I should like to go back to this scene on foot; for I had no idea that there was such a region within a few miles of us.

By and by, we saw Monument Mountain, and Rattlesnake hill, and all the familiar features of our own landscape, except the lake, which (by some witchcraft that I cannot possibly explain to myself) had utterly vanished. It appeared as if we ought to see the lake, and our little red-house, and Highwood; but none of these objects were discoverable, although the scene was certainly that of which they make a part. It was now after sunset; and we found that as we went we were approaching the village of Lenox from the west, and must pass through it before reaching home. I got out at the post office, and received, among other things, a letter from Phoebe. By the time we were out of the village, it was beyond twilight; indeed, but for the full moon, it would have been quite dark. The little man behaved himself still like an old traveller; but sometimes he looked round at me from the front seat (where he sat between Herman Melville and Evert Duyckinck) and smiled at me with a peculiar expression, and put back his hand to touch me. It was a method of establishing a sympathy in what doubtless appeared to him the wildest and unprecedentedest series of adventures that had ever befallen mortal travellers. Anon, we drew up at the little gate of the old red house.

Now, with many doubts as to the result, but constrained by the necessity of the case, I had asked the party to take tea and rest the horses, before returning to Pittsfield. I did not know but Mrs. Peters would absolutely refuse to co-operate, at such an hour, and with such poor means as were at hand. However, she bestirred herself at once, like a colored angel as she is; and for my own part, I went over to Highwood, a humble suppliant for some loaf sugar and for whatever else Mrs. Tappan should be pleased to bestow. She too showed herself angelically disposed, and gave me not only the sugar, but a pot of raspberry jam, and some little bread-cakes—an inestimable gift, inasmuch as our own bread was sour.

Immediately on our arrival, Julian had flung himself on the couch, without so much as taking off his hat, and fallen asleep. When I got back from Highwood, I found that Mrs. Peters had already given him his supper, and that he was munching his final piece of bread. So I undressed him, and asked him, meanwhile, whether he had had a good time. But the naughty little man said "no"; whereas, until within the last half hour, never had he been happier in his life; but this latter weariness had effaced the memory of all that enjoyment. I never saw such self gratulation and contentment as that wherewith he stretched himself out in bed, and doubtless was asleep before I reached the foot of the stairs.

In a little while more, Mrs. Peters had supper ready— no very splendid supper, but not nearly so meagre as it might have been. Tea, bread and butter, dropt eggs, little bread-cakes, raspberry jam; and I truly thanked Heaven, and Mrs. Peters, that it was no worse! After tea, we had a smoke, and some pleasant conversation; and at ten o'clock the guests departed. I looked over one or two newspapers, and went to bed before eleven. It was a most beautiful night, with full, rich, cloudless moonlight, so that I would rather have ridden the six miles to Pittsfield, than have gone to bed.

SATURDAY, AUGUST 9TH, [1851].

———

Julian awoke in bright condition, this morning; and we arose at about seven. I felt the better for the expedition of yesterday; and asking Julian whether he had a good time, he answered with great enthusiasm in the affirmative, and that he wanted to go again, and that he loved Mr. Melville as well as me, and as mamma, and as Una.

It being so fair and fine weather, last night, it followed as a matter of course that it should be showery, this morning; and so it was. The rain was pouring when we got up; and though it held up when I went for the milk, the atmosphere was very vaporish and juicy. From all the hill sides mists were steaming up, and Monument Mountain seemed to be enveloped as if in the smoke of a great battle. I kept Julian within doors till about eleven, when, the sun glimmering out, we went to the barn, and afterwards to the garden. The rest of the time, he has played at jack-straws, and ridden on his horse, and through all and above all, has deafened and confounded me with his interminable babble. I read him, in the course of the morning, a portion of his mother's letter that was addressed to himself; and he chuckled immeasurably.

We could not venture away from the house and its environment, on account of the weather; and so we got rid of the day as well as we could, within those precincts. I think I have hardly ever known Julian talk so incessantly as he has to-day; if I did not attend to him, he talked to himself. He has been in excellent spirits all the time.

Between four and five o'clock, came on one of the heaviest showers of the day; and in the midst of it, there was a succession of thundering knocks at the front door.

Julian and I ran as quickly as possible to see whom it might be; and on opening the door, there was a young man on the door step, and a carriage at the gate, and Mr. James thrusting his head out of the carriage window, and beseeching shelter from the storm! So here was an invasion. Mr. & Mrs. James, their eldest son, their daughter, their little son Charles, their maid-servant, and their coachman;—not that the coachman came in; and as for the maid, she staid in the hall. Dear me, where was Phoebe in this time of need! All taken aback as I was, I made the best of it. Julian helped me somewhat, but not much. Little Charley is a few months younger than he, and between them, they at least furnished subject for remark. Mrs. James, luckily, seemed to be very much afraid of thunder and lightning; and as these were loud and sharp, she might be considered *hors du combat*. The son, who seemed to be about twenty, and the daughter, of seventeen or eighteen, took the part of saying nothing; which I suppose is the English fashion, as regards such striplings. So Mr. James was the only one to whom it was necessary to talk; and we got along tolerably well. He said that this was his birth-day, and that he was keeping it by a pleasure-excursion, and that therefore the rain was a matter of course. We talked of periodicals, English and American, and of the Puritans, about whom we agreed pretty well in our opinions; and Mr. James told how he had been recently thrown out of his wagon, and how the horse ran away with Mrs. James;—and we talked about green lizards and red ones. And Mr. James told Julian how, when he was a child, he had twelve owls at the same time, and, at another time, a raven, who used to steal silver spoons and money; he also mentioned a squirrel, and various other pets—and Julian laughed most obstreperously.

As to little Charley, he was much interested with Bunny, and likewise with the rocking-horse, which luckily happened to be in the sitting-room. He examined the horse most critically, and asked a thousand questions about him, with a particularly distinct utterance, and not the slightest bashfulness; finally, he got upon the horse's back, but did not show himself quite so good a rider as Julian. Our old boy hardly said a word; indeed it could hardly be expected, on the first brunt of such an irruption as we were undergoing. Finally, the shower past over, and the invaders passed away; and I do hope, that, on the next occasion of the kind, my wife may be there to see.

Immediately on their departure, Mrs. Peters brought in Julian's supper; being in a hurry to arrange matters and go home. It is now twenty minutes past six.

I spent a rather forlorn evening, and to bed at nine.

SUNDAY, AUGUST 10TH, [1851].

Uprose we at not much after six. It was a particularly cool and north-west windy morning; and sullen and angry clouds were scattered about, especially to the northward. When we went for the milk, Luther Butler expressed his opinion that Indian corn would not do very well, this season. In fact, it hardly seems like a summer at all.

I got the breakfast, and the morning passed away without any incident, till about ten, when we set out for the lake. There the little man took an old branch of a tree, and set very earnestly to fishing. Such perseverance certainly does deserve a better reward than it is likely to meet with; although he seems to enjoy it, and always comes away without any apparent disappointment. Afterwards, we threw stones into the lake; and I lay on the bank, under the trees, and watched his little busyness—his never-wearying activity—as cheerful as the sun, and shedding a reflected cheer upon my sombreness. From the lake, we strolled upward, fighting mulleins and thistles, and I sat down on the edge of the tall pine wood. He finds so much to amuse him in every possible spot we light upon, that he always contends stoutly against a removal. After spending a little time here, we passed through the wood, to the field beyond, where he insisted that I should sit down on a great rock, and let him dig in the sand; and so I did. Here the old boy made little holes, and heaped up the sand, and imagined his constructions to be fairy houses; and I believe he would willingly have spent the rest of the day there, had I been as content as he. We came homeward by the cold spring, out of which we drank; and when we reached the house, it was after one.

For dinner, I gave him bread and water, and a small remnant of corn-starch pudding; and I myself ate a piece of cake and a cucumber. Then we went out and fed the hens; after which I lay down on the slope of the valley, and smoked a cigar, with the sun falling upon me out of the clear blue sky, warm and genial, but with not too heavy a warmth. Julian, meanwhile, played about, not so far off as to lose the feeling of companionship, yet so far that he could only speak to me in a shout; and whenever he shouted, a child's clear voice, in the distance, shouted more faintly the self-same words. It was the echo. And thus we have arrived at half past two. The old boy is now riding on his rocking-horse, and talking to me as fast as his tongue can go. Mercy on me, was ever man before so be-pelted with a child's talk as I am! It is his desire of sympathy that lies at the bottom of the great heap of his babblement. He wants to enrich all his enjoyments by steeping them in the heart of some friend. I do not think him in danger of living so solitary a life as much of mine has been.

During the afternoon, we gathered some currants, which I crushed, and gave him a few at supper. When that was over (and we got through with it before six) we went out to the barn. "A very fine morning, isn't it, father?" said he, as we came out of the door. I wish I could record all his apothegms; but they do not seem worth writing down, till I have so far forgotten them that they cannot be recalled in their integrity. To-day, after beating down a great many thistles, he observed,—"All the world is a great pricker!" He has an idea that I do not think him very wise; and this afternoon he asked—"Father, do you think I don't know anything?"—"I do," said I. "But I knew how to shut the boudoir-door, when you didn't," rejoined he. I am very glad he has that one instance of practical sagacity (though after all it was merely a chance hit) to console himself with. Nevertheless, I really think he has the stuff in him to make wisdom of, in due season; and Heaven forbid that it should come too soon.

At bed-time, I indulged him in what he likes better than almost anything else—a rampageous sham-battle—before undressing him; and at seven o'clock, he was finally stowed away. Let me say outright, for once, that he is a sweet and lovely little boy, and worthy of all the love that I am capable of giving him. Thank God! God bless him! God bless Phoebe for giving him to me! God bless her as the best wife and mother in the world! God bless Una, whom I long to see again! God bless little Rosebud! God bless me, for Phoebe's and all their sakes! No other man has so good a wife; nobody has better children. Would I were worthier of her and them!

My evenings are all dreary, alone, and without books that I am in the mood to read; and this evening was like the rest. So I went to bed at about nine, and longed for Phoebe.

MONDAY, AUGUST 11TH, [1851].

The little man spoke to me, sometime in the depth of night, and said very quietly that he did not have very pleasant dreams. Doubtless, the currants, which he ate at supper, had wrought a malevolent influence upon him; and, in fact, I could hear them rumbling in his belly. He himself heard the rumor of them, but did not recognize where the sound came from, and inquired of me what it was. After a while, he fell asleep again, and slept some-what later than usual; insomuch that I arose at not far from seven, bathed, and finally had to arouse him. Mrs. Peters returned before his bath was over. He munched a slice of bread, as we went together for the milk. It was a clear, calm, and pretty cool morning.

After breakfast, I gathered some string beans, and good store of summer-squashes; then frizzled the old gentleman's wig, and went up stairs to my own toilet. Before ten, we set out on a walk along the mountain-side, by the Hudson-road. There could not be more delightful weather; warm, but not too warm, except in the full brunt of the sunbeams—and a gently stirring breeze, which had the memory of an ice-berg in it; as all the breezes of this summer have. It was a very pleasant walk. The old boy (who well merits to be dubbed a Knight of the Thistle) performed feats of valor against these old enemies; neither did I shrink from the combat. He found many flowers, too, and was enthusiastic about their beauty; often bestowing his encomiums on very homely ones. But he has a real feeling for everything that grows. In the wood opposite Mr. Flint's, we saw some men cutting down trees; at which he expressed great anger, and said he would rather have no fire, and drink cold milk. We walked a good way along the road, until we came within sight of a house, which stands at what seems to be the highest point, and deepest in the forest. Thence we turned back, and rested ourselves on some logs, a little withdrawn from the roadside. The little man said that one of these logs was Giant Despair, and that the old giant was dead; and he dug a shallow hole, which he said should be the giant's grave. I objected that it was not half large enough; but he informed me that Giant Despair grew very small, the moment he was dead.

While we sat here, a man passed in a four wheeled chaise; and soon afterwards came a handsome barouche and pair, with two ladies and a whiskered gentleman in it, making a very gay spectacle along the forest-road; and in the other direction came a wagon, driven by a boy, and containing a woman and a little girl, who, I suppose, were his mother and sister. The woman alighted, and coming towards me, asked if I had seen any stray chickens! It seems, in passing over the road, this morning, they had lost some chickens out of the wagon, and now were seeking them; but in my opinion, they might have called wild birds out of the trees, with about as much hope of success. However, when we came away, they were still seeking their chickens, and the boy was calling "Chick, chick, chick!" with something lamentable in his tone; and for aught I know, he is calling them yet; but the chickens have strayed into the wild wood, and will perhaps intermarry with partridges, or establish a race of wild hens. Julian and I came homeward, more slowly than we went; for the sun had grown pretty fervent, and our walk had been quite a long one. We found high-bush blackberries along the way, but I allowed him to eat only a very few;

and therefore gained most of the little handfulls, which he gathered, for my own eating. It was about twelve when we reached the house.

He has had peculiar longings for his mother and Una to-day, and pronounces his love for them with great emphasis. I do not think he has given Rosebud any place in his affections yet; though he answered—"Yes"—in a matter of course way, when I inquired whether he did not love her too. It is now about half past two, and he wishes to take a walk to the lake.

We went accordingly; and there he took a bare pole and set to fishing again—poor, patient little angler that he is! I lay a long while on the green margin of the lake, partly in the shade and partly in the sun. The breeze seemed to come from the southward, and was pretty brisk; so that it sang among the trees, and heaved the wavelets against the shore. I almost fell asleep; but whenever I unclosed my eyes, there was the unweariable fisher-boy. By-and-by, he proposed to go to "Mother's Rock," as he has named a certain large rock, beneath some walnut-trees, where the children went with Phoebe to gather nuts, last autumn. He informed me that, when he was grown up, he should build a house for his mother, at this rock, and that I might live there too. "When I am grown up," he said, "every-body must mind me!" We visited "Mother's Rock"; and then he picked up the nuts of last year, and perseveringly cracked them, believing that in every one he should find good meats—nor yet seeming to feel much disappointed, when he found them all decayed. We spent some time here, and then came home through the pasture; and the little man kept jumping over the high weeds, and the tufts of everlasting flowers;—while I compared his overflowing sprightliness with my own reluctant footsteps, and was content that he should be young instead of I. We got home at about five.

I have just put the old fellow to bed, at a quarter of seven. He expressed some fear that he should have the bad dream of last night, over again; but I told him, that, as he had eaten no currants to-night, he would not probably be troubled. He says the dream was about dogs.

To bed at about nine.

TUESDAY, AUGUST 12TH, [1851].

Up at a little past six. The old gentleman said that he had had a very pleasant night, and no dreams. For myself, I seemed to toss and tumble about, the whole night through;—which is the stranger, as I ate not a mouthfull of supper. The morning was warm, with a partially over-cast sky, and mist on the hills. The sun gleamed out, as we were going for the milk, but quickly withdrew him-self again. Julian capered along, in the best imaginable spirits. He makes a very funny little figure, this week; his drawers being particularly short, so that a great deal of bare leg is visible, some of which is tanned brown, while the rest is white.

When I came down from dressing, after breakfast, I found a letter from Phoebe on the table, fixing her return on Thursday. Julian has taken a notion that she is to come back tomorrow, and he will not be persuaded out of it.

At about eleven, we took our well-worn walk to the lake; where of course, the old gentleman resumed his piscatory pastime. It would have been an excellent day for real fishing, with its stillness and cloudiness; but before we left the lake, the breeze stirred and ruffled its surface. It was nearly dinner-time when we returned; but the little man had to be appeased with a slice of bread, preliminarily, and afterwards feasted immensely on rice, squash, and string-beans. After dinner, I sat down with a book in the boudoir; and, for the first time since his mother went away, he was absent in parts unknown, for the space of an hour. At last I began to think it time to look him up; for, now that I am alone with him, I have all his mother's anxieties, added to my own. So I went to the barn, and to the currant-bushes, and shouted around the house, without response, and finally sat down on the hay, not knowing which way to seek him. But by and by, he ran round the house, holding up his little fist, with a smiling phiz, and crying out that he had something very good for me. The "something good" proved to be a squeezed up pulp, consisting of raspberries, blackberries, and gooseberries, which had been stewing in his fist for an hour past; a kind of cookery for which his mother would have thought them all the better. I could not find in my heart utterly to refuse his gift; so I took a few of the gooseberries, which happened not to be crushed, and allowed him to eat the rest; for he said that he had not tasted one.

It being by this time four o'clock, I dressed him and myself, and we set out for the village. There were a few clouds, which sometimes kindly came across the sun; but it seemed to be the sultriest day of the whole summer, and I really suffered with the heat—a heavy, brooding, oppressive heat. At the village, I found a note from E. P. P.; another from Longfellow, and one from a lady requesting an autograph. On our way home, the little man was so weary and hot that he wished me to carry him, and declared that he never wanted to go to the village again, nor even to the lake. It was indeed a most wearisome walk. And now, at seven o'clock, I am going to put him to bed.

Being in the garden, after putting Julian to-bed, Mrs.

Tappan passed along the road, and asked me to go home with her and see whether she had any books which I would like. So I went, and took a number of Harper's Magazine, and one or two other periodicals. I had brought her a letter from Ellery Channing, in which he proposes a visit; but she is going to decline it, for the present, on account of want of room, and there being a baby in the house. She inquired, with apparent seriousness, whether we could not receive his visit!!!—our house being so much bigger than hers, and we having no baby. I looked over the periodicals till half past nine, and then to bed.

WEDNESDAY, AUGUST 13TH, [1851].

The little man did not bestir himself so early as usual; so at last I got up, after being some time awake, and found it to be nearly seven o'clock. I bathed, before calling him. It was an overcast morning, with mists sleeping heavily on all the hills; but here and there, you could see the sunbeams melting through them, and there was every prospect of a hot and shining day. I suppose this mist and cloudiness is merely local; so that Phoebe will probably have a fair morning, in which to start for home. After all, Julian seems to have been right in his obstinate declaration that his mother was to return to-day. He appears now to have given up the idea, however, and to acquiesce in her delaying till tomorrow. His mind is full of the subject, nevertheless; and seeing me in a clean pair of linen pantaloons, just now, he asked if I had put them on for mamma. As we were going for the milk, he talked about what his delight would be, and how he should behave, when his mother arrived; but on our way home, he talked of Una, and how she had troubled him, and what he should do in case of further troubles. I doubt that the poor little man ever had quite so quiet a time as he has had with me—or ever will have such another.

At ten o'clock, we took a stroll in Tanglewood, without any adventure, and returned at eleven. The remainder of the forenoon, we have spent in the house; it being very warm, and Julian disinclined to move. He complains of not feeling well, but cannot describe his symptoms. I rather think dinner will set him right. In the meantime, as the best prescription I can think of, I have given him a dose of aconite. His bowels do not seem to be at all out of order. Our hot and weary walk, yesterday, may have affected him.

After dinner, we went out and sat under the trees, for awhile; and have spent the rest of the afternoon in the house; except that the little man went out to see a load of hay pitched into the barn, and afterwards took a short ride on the haycart. At five o'clock, he complained that his head ached, and I gave him a dose of Belladonna. Towards evening, he brightened up, ate a good supper, and seemed altogether as well as usual. Indeed, he has not appeared decidedly unwell, at any moment. At seven, he engaged with great spirit in his beloved sham-battle, and is now in bed. I did hope (relying undoubtingly on E. P. P.'s letter) that he would have seen his mother, before he slept to-night.

I looked over a periodical, during the evening, and went to bed at nine.

THURSDAY, AUGUST 14TH, [1851].

I had a very long waking spell, in the mid of night, and fell asleep towards morning; and the little man awoke earlier than I. After some little delay, we both got up, and found it to be not yet six. He seemed quite bright and in good condition.

Going for the milk, we saw a dim rainbow; there being

a scarcely perceptible shower, and the sun shining out faintly, at the same time. I fear, from subsequent and present appearances, that it was prophetic of bad weather for the day. The old gentleman philosophized about rainbows, as we went along; but I remember nothing that he said, except that the sunshine was the light of the rainbow. At breakfast, he got astride of a fantasy, and said how he would go up among the clouds, and brush them away; so that his mother might have fair weather to come home in. He announced, too, that he should set up Monument mountain on its end, the longest way, for the purpose, I believe, of climbing up to the clouds upon it. Observing some cake which Mrs. Peters had set on the table for me, he became discontented with his own breakfast, and wanted something different from the ordinary bread and milk. I told him that his bread, this morning, had yeast in it; and he forthwith began to eat it with a great appetite, and thought it better than he ever tasted.

About an hour after breakfast, he was afflicted with the stomach-ache; and I gave him some pulsatilla. It appeared to be a pretty severe, but ineffectual griping, and not to be followed by any consequences. It has now passed away, and he is looking over the German picture-book, in excellent spirits. The day has apparently taken a settled character for cloud and sullenness, at least, if not for absolute inclemency. Still, I do not know but it will be more comfortable for Phoebe's journey, than the sultriness of yesterday. Would she were here! It is now half past nine; and in eight hours more, it will be time to hearken for her chariot-wheels.

It being chill and cloudy, we spent the forenoon entirely in the house. The old boy has been very happy; amusing himself with cutting paper, looking at pictures, riding on his horse, and all the time prating to me—without a moment of ill-humor (which, indeed, is hardly among his possibilities) or ill spirits. His stomach-ache has not returned. He ate a good dinner of maccaroni, rice, squash, and bread; and I hope his mother will be here before night, to receive him from my hands in perfect order, and to be delighted with the babble which, for nearly three weeks past, has run like a brook through all my thoughts. He does not anticipate her return very vividly to-day. He has not an intense conception of "soon," or "now," any more than of any other time. For my part, I shall be bitterly disappointed if she does not come to-night.

At three, or a little later, Julian insisted so earnestly that we should go down to the lake, that I had to comply, especially as the sun had come out pretty decidedly. So away we went; and the mannikin was in the highest possible exhilaration, absolutely tumbling down with laughter, once or twice, at small cause. On reaching the lake, he sobered himself and began to angle, with all the staidness of an ancient fisherman. By this time, it had clouded over again; and the lake looked wild and angry, as the gusts swept over it. I feared it might be too chill for the old gentleman to remain long at his present quiescent occupation; and so I soon called him away, and we fought our way home through those never-failing enemies, the thistles. It is now nearly five; and within an hour, surely, or very little more, Phoebe cannot fail to shine upon us. It seems absolutely an age since she departed. I think I hear the sound of wheels now. It was not she.

Julian has just cried out "Oh, I wish mother would come! I want to see her so much!—to see her!—to see her!—to see her! Father, perhaps we shall find Rose grown up when we see her again!"

Inconceivable to tell, she did not come! I put Julian to bed not long after six, and then set out for the Post office. It was a clear and beautiful sunset, with a brisk, Septembrish temperature. To my further astoundment, I found no letter; so that I conclude she must have intended to come to-day. It may be that there was a decided rain, this morning, in the region roundabout Boston, and that this prevented her setting out. I met Mrs. Tappan, just before reaching home; and she said that Mr. Ward, who was to have taken Phoebe and the children under his escort, has not arrived. Not improbably, the cause of the delay lies with him.

I read the paper during the evening, by very dim lamp-light, and went to bed at half past nine.

FRIDAY, AUGUST 15TH, [1851].

—

We did not get up till seven o'clock this morning. It was very clear, and of autumnal freshness, with a breeze from the north-west. I put a knit-jacket on the old gentleman, when we went for the milk; but I fear his poor little bare legs, in the intervals between his stockings and drawers, must have felt rather bleak. However, he trudged along in brisk spirits, and tumbled down three times in the course of the walk. On our way home, we met three ladies on horseback, attended by a gentleman; and the little man asked me whether I thought the ladies pretty, and said that he did not. They really were rather pretty, in my opinion; but I suspect that their appearance on horseback did not suit his taste; and I agree with him that a woman is a monstrous and disagreeable spectacle, in such an atti-tude. But the old boy is very critical in matters of beauty; although I think that the real ground of his censures usu-ally lies in some wrong done to his sense of fitness and propriety. But this sense is sometimes conventional with him. For instance, he denied that the Quaker lady, who called on me, was pretty; and it turned out that he did not like the unaccustomed fashion of her dress, and her thees and thous.

At ten o'clock, we set out on a walk towards the lake. All the way, and during the whole excursion, Julian was full of Giant Despair, and attributed all his mishaps to that malevolent personage. He happened to tread in some fresh "cow-mud," as Una calls it; and he said that the giant had made it there, so as to trouble him. When we came to the open part of Shadow Brook, I lay down on the bank, full exposed to the sun, and basked there, with a pleasant sense of too much warmth; while sometimes a breath of wind would find its way there, and refresh me with its austerity. And here I smoked a cigar; partly here, and partly on the shore of the lake. It is a perfect forenoon of its kind, only it comes just about a month too soon. Julian fished, as usual, in the lake, and afterwards threw stones in it, and seemed never to be weary of haunting its margin, any more than a kingfisher which we often see there, flitting from one decayed branch to another. But I grew tired, after a while, and insisted on returning home; whither we arrived at precisely noon.

It is now half past four. We have made no other excursion to-day, but have loitered in and about the house.

Julian does not appear to have any imminent impression of his mother's coming though once or twice he has said what a good day it was for her to come. Perhaps she is by this time in the village. I feel as if she were coming; but after previous disappointments, I do not look upon it as a certainty. Julian, by the by, seems perfectly well; but, I must say, his hair has taken a worse aspect, to-day, than anytime during her absence; and yet I frizzled it as carefully as I could. He has on his knit woollen jacket, too, which disfigures him horribly; but he will not be persuaded to dispense with it; so his mother, I suppose, will think he has been looking like a fright, ever since she went away.

Bunny is evidently out of order. He appeared to be indisposed, yesterday, and is still more evidently so, to-day. He has just had a shivering fit. Julian thinks he has the scarlet fever; that being the only disease with which he has ever been conversant.

Mr. Ward has just been here (at half past five) expecting to find that Phoebe had arrived yesterday. This heightens the mystery. E. P. P. wrote me that he would escort her on Wednesday. He was prevented from coming on that day, but supposed that she would have come with Mrs. Minott, on Thursday. Where can she be?

I put Julian to bed very soon after supper, and immediately set-out for the village. Still no letter from Sophia. I think she must have been under some mistake as to Mr. Ward's movements, and has waited in expectation of his escort. There was a great box, directed to me, at the Post Office, which probably contains her Boston purchases. Returning home, I spent the evening in reading newspapers. In one of them (the N.Y. Evening Post) I saw an account of the Commencement at the Wesleyan University, Middletown, Conn.; and one of the Baccalaureate exercises was a "Modern Classical Oration," by Edwin Holsey Cole, of Cromwell, on myself! I don't quite understand the nature of the performance, and whether it was in Latin or the vernacular; but I should have been curious to hear it.

To bed, disconsolate, at a little before ten.

SATURDAY, AUGUST 16TH, [1851].

The little man awoke before day, and continued awake sometime, of course keeping me awake too; but fell asleep after a good while, and slept till nearly seven—when we both got up. On entering the bathing-room, I peeped into Bunny's box, with something like a foreboding of what had happened; and sure enough, there lay the poor little beast, stark and stiff. That shivering fit, yesterday, had a very fatal aspect in my eyes. I have no idea what was his disorder; his digestive functions appeared to be all right, and his symptoms had been merely a disinclination, for the last two days, to move or eat. Julian seemed to be interested and excited by the event, rather than afflicted. He imputed it, as he does all other mishaps, to the agency of Giant Despair; and, as we were going for the milk, he declared it was the wickedest thing the giant ever did— "more wickeder" than when he made the cow-mud.

After breakfast, I dug a hole, and we planted poor Bunny in the garden; and the old gentleman expressed his hopes that, by tomorrow, a flower will have sprung up over him. After frizzling Julian's wig, and shaving myself, I sent him over to Highwood with a note to Mrs. Tappan, informing her of the great box at the Post Office, and suggesting that it probably contained her rice, and hinting the little probability that she would ever get it, unless by sending the wagon for the box. This being the proper method of presenting the affair, she saw it in the right light, and told Julian she would send. It is now nearly ten, and Julian is teazing me to go to the lake. He says, just now—"Perhaps tomorrow there will be a tree of Bunnies, and they will hang all over it by their ears!" I have before this observed, that children have an odd propensity to treat death (the deaths of animals, at least) as a joke, though rather nervously. He has laughed a good deal about Bunny's exit.

We went to the lake, in accordance with the old boy's wish. He had taken with him the little vessel that his Uncle Nat made for him, long ago, and which since yesterday has been his favorite plaything. He launched it upon the lake, and it looked very like a real sloop, tossing up and down on the swelling waves. I believe he would very contentedly have spent a hundred years, or so, with no other amusement than this. I, meanwhile, took the National Era from my pocket, and gave it a pretty attentive perusal. I have before now experienced, that the best way to get a vivid impression and feeling of a landscape, is to sit down before it and read, or become otherwise absorbed in thought; for then, when your eyes happen to be attracted to the landscape, you seem to catch Nature at unawares, and see her before she has time to change her aspect. The effect lasts but for a single instant, and passes away almost as soon as you are conscious of it; but it is real, for that moment. It is as if you could overhear and understand what the trees are whispering to one another; as if you caught a glimpse of a face unveiled, which veils itself from every wilful glance. The mystery is revealed, and after a breath or two, becomes just as much a mystery as before. I caught one such glimpse, this forenoon, though not so perfectly as sometimes. It was half past twelve when we got back.

I forgot to say that I left a note for Mr. Steele, at the Post Office, requesting him to wait in Pittsfield for Phoebe. If she does not come to-day,—well, I don't know what I shall do.

It is nearly six by the clock, and they do not come! Surely, they must, must, must be here to-night!

Within a quarter of an hour after writing the above, they have come—all well! Thank God.

NATHANIEL HAWTHORNE (1804–1864) was born in Salem, Massachusetts. He was a young child when his father, a sea captain, died, and his mother retreated into a state of seclusion and mourning that lasted for the rest of her long life. After graduating from Bowdoin College in 1825, Hawthorne returned to Salem, where he wrote historical sketches and allegorical tales, as well as a novel, *Fanshawe*, which was published anonymously in 1828. His first book of stories, *Twice-Told Tales*, appeared in 1837 and was expanded in 1842. Hawthorne worked for some years as the editor of *The American Magazine of Useful and Entertaining Knowledge*, as a hack writer, and in the Boston and Salem offices of the US Customs. His marriage to Sophia Peabody, in 1842, led to a move to Concord, after which he wrote the stories gathered in *Mosses From an Old Manse* (1846) and *The Snow-Image, and Other Twice-Told Tales* (1852), and the novels *The Scarlet Letter* (1850), *The House of the Seven Gables* (1851), and *The Blithedale Romance* (1852). During these same years Hawthorne also spent time in the Berkshires (the scene of *Twenty Days with Julian & Little Bunny*), where he struck up a friendship with his young admirer Herman Melville. In 1852 Hawthorne's old friend Franklin Pierce was elected president of the United States, and Hawthorne, who had written Pierce's campaign biography, was rewarded with a consulship in Liverpool. Four years in England were followed by another two in Italy, after which Hawthorne returned with his family to Concord. His last novel, *The Marble Faun*, was published in 1860.

PAUL AUSTER is the author of ten novels, most recently *The Book of Illusions*. He lives with his wife and daughter in Brooklyn.

...crushed, and gave him a fe...
...ed can got through with it a...
...em. "A very fine morning,...
...me out of the door. I wish...
...gus; but they do not seem...
...few forgotten them that they...
...rity. To-day, after beaten...
...observed, — "All the world...
...idea that I do not thin...
...was he asked — "Paper,...
...ything?" "I do," said...
...boudoir-door, when ...
...y glad he has that one inten...
...ter all it was merely a ...
...ith. Nevertheless, I really ...